Mantras

TOOLS *for the* MIND

This disempowers your issues. When you hold their absence as the all-powerful clue of your progress, you have given them way too much power. Take your judgments about yourself off the pedestal and bring them down to a human level. It's just your stuff, like everybody else has their stuff, this is part of your agenda. It's not off your path to be working with your petty issues; it's simply part of it.

When jealousy, envy, petty anger, judgments, etc., arise, see them as the current field of consciousness that your soul needs to work with at this time. Instead of being distraught for having the petty issues in the first place, you see them as the current issues your soul needs you to work on for your growth. By accepting your issues, they are easier to tame and will continue to become increasingly more subtle.

Kundalini

KUNDALINI IS A principle from Hindu philosophy that is helpful for understanding this process of moving the energy up through the chakras. Basically, Kundalini means "serpent power." Kundalini energy is coiled at the base of the spine. Through different situations, exercises and meditations the kundalini uncoils and moves up the series of chakras, releasing the energy stored in each chakra it contacts. This method of visualization offers us an image of understanding the process of awakening to the surge of energy released in the upper chakras.

Kundalini experiences can happen spontaneously, where you simply seem to fall into the release of this incredible energy—quite by chance. To experience the surges of energy of the upper chakras is one thing when that is what you are trying to do, but it is quite another thing when a person has no preparation or training for handling the awakened energy. Most often, when people are talking about Kundalini energy, it is problematic. Crazy energy: rushes, twitches, heat, anxiety attacks, too much energy. These are all clues the energy isn't being balanced.

The Kundalini has risen beyond the ability to handle the energy and the crazy energy is essentially a "shooting out"

Published by Jaico Publishing House
A-2 Jash Chambers, 7-A Sir Phirozshah Mehta Road
Fort, Mumbai - 400 001
jaicopub@jaicobooks.com
www.jaicobooks.com

MANTRAS: TOOLS FOR THE MIND
ISBN 978-93-89305-03-6

Original English language edition published as
Mantras for Peace of Mind

Jaico Print-on-Demand Edition: 2025

Page design and layout: Jojy Philip, Delhi

Printed by
Repro India Limited, Mumbai

A Myth

WE ARE THE Counsel of Seven and you will be hearing more from us as more of you awaken to full consciousness. We are nothing more than the collective wisdom of humanity. As each of you awaken to full consciousness, and your role within humanity, our voice gets stronger. To listen to our guidance the rules are simple—that which unites will lead you to us and that which separates will lead you astray. To listen to the universal mind, adopt a universal philosophy. We would like to tell you a story.

A long, long time ago, when we were all still light beings existing in spirit but not in form, our tribe of angels was exploring the universe for opportunities to serve. We were on a fly-by of planet earth and noticed all the suffering occurring there. Here was a planet of tremendous beauty beyond compare in all of the universe, yet it was encased in a shroud of fear that limited the inhabitants in their ability to realize what a gift their lovely planet was.

Our leaders looked down upon the situation and, with compassion, thought this was a planet that certainly needed cosmic assistance to bring it into the love vibration. It was suggested that perhaps we would like to go down to earth

Foreword

In this human birth, we cultivate many relationships. We share special relationships with some of our family members: our favourite sister, brother or aunt, for instance. We take pains to build an effective rapport with superiors and colleagues. We do all this, motivated by personal gain or to satisfy our inherent needs for emotional security, genuine affection and respect.

This is all very well, but there is one relationship that we must not neglect amid all these worldly links – our special and unique relationship with God. For this reason, I constantly urge my friends, "Make God real in your daily life! Cultivate a special and loving relationship with Him! Let this bond grow stronger and stronger with each day of your life!"

Let me tell you that cultivating a personal relationship with God is not as difficult and abstract as it may sound. God is not far from us, He does not live on a distant planet. He is nearer to you than your friends or family and closer than your breath! In the endless adventure of existence, God and man are comrades. God is the one unfailing companion, who will never leave us. We may try to run away from Him, but He will continue to follow us like our own shadow. In the paths to identify specific karmic indicators that the soul needed to deal with, heal and integrate, and this healing was not difficult with the assistance of spirit.

At first, these visionaries were accused of being "airy-fairy," ungrounded in reality, space cadets, until they were able to demonstrate their truth. As more and more individuals successfully used the maps to heal old wounds and move into cooperation with spirit, the example of their lives became a model of what was possible. The demonstration of a life guided by spirit and nurtured by soul grew, and these visionaries became living examples that others could follow. Their love was so much stronger than fear, that once these individuals woke up to the full remembrance of their purpose, they became as a light in the darkness that could help others to see.

This story need not be a fairy tale. We do tremendous service by advising others of their possibilities, but the greatest legacy that we will leave behind is the life we live ourselves. Physician, heal thyself. Live your truth. If we are to be a powerful influence in healing this planet, then it is we ourselves that must demonstrate this in how we live our lives. We have the maps for integration. We can live a life of health in body, mind, spirit and soul. By doing so, we are grounding the vision of our spiritual leaders and creating a light for others to follow.

SECTION IV

Exercises and Meditations

If these reflections should draw some of you closer to God and give you peace, the purpose of this little collection would be more than fulfilled!

Visualization Exercise

MOST OFTEN I prefer to use meditation and visualizations for aligning with the energy I want to experience. There are, however, methods for using visualization to remove unwanted energies. The following is a good example for doing just that.

Exercise 11

For Filtering Out Unwanted Energies: First get in a meditative state and activate each of the chakras through one of the chakra meditations. Next, visualize a screen in front of you, like a large screen door. Then, imagine yourself moving through that screen and imagine that all unwanted energies attached to you—worries, fears, expectations from others, etc., are filtered out as you move through the screen.

As you picture yourself on the other side of the screen, feel what it is like to be your most genuine self without any unnatural energies attached to you. Walk through another screen in your mind's eye with even a finer mesh and see yourself purified of all that is not your true essence. Walk through as many screens as it takes until you see the colors of your aura as pure, and radiating a brilliant light.

mantras can also be described as 'energy-based sounds' that are capable of elevating our consciousness. To create such potent sound vibrations, correct pronunciation and chanting of the mantra are very essential.

According to Sri Swami Satyananda, the etymological meaning of the word mantra is "by repetition of which the mind becomes free from external experiences." Mantras are not simply syllables or words, but mystic sounds that were revealed to rishis or seers while in deep states of meditation. These mantras have been handed down from Guru to disciple for thousands of years. "Such mantras," says Sri Swamiji, "can completely explode the whole personality and open the gates to higher awareness."

Many other faiths like Buddhism, Jainism and Sikhism also accentuate the power of the mantra. For example, the Dalai Lama asserts in one of his books that "without depending upon mantra... Buddhahood cannot be attained." The sacred *Guru Granth Sahib* tells us: "I have found the Perfect Guru, through great good fortune; He has given me the Mantra of the Lord's Name, and my mind has become quiet and tranquil."

Surely it is with good reason that so many faiths and so many scriptures profess the power of a mantra!

- Mantras are sacred *shabdas* or sounds; they produce positive, healing vibrations that bring tranquility to the mind and promote spiritual progress.
- They create positive energy, which emanates from both the articulation as well as the intent and faith with which they are uttered.
- Many mantras have their own meanings, but their general effect transcends the semantic or literal.

Practitioners tell us that the true meaning of any mantra can only be realized through the effect that is created by its constant repetition.

- Mantras are linked to the highest levels of our consciousness. They elevate our thinking and awareness, awakening what is called the kundalini shakti in us.
- Mantras have been described as 'tools of power and tools for power', based on the definition above. They discipline and free the mind from vagaries and impure thoughts; they give the mind the power to focus as well as concentrate, so as to render it an invaluable instrument of the spirit.

Those who are beginners can also reap the immense benefit of the mantra's healing power. Simply concentrate on a mantra, a holy name, a word or syllable, which to you is symbolic of God or Truth (the shorter the mantra, the better). Repeat it again and again in a musical manner. Repeat it with the deep love and longing of the heart. Repeat it until it gets engraved on your mind and is in the background of your consciousness all the time, even while you work or sleep.

God is the Nameless One: the sages have called Him by many Names because of his omnipresence. The numerous mantras, holy names, words or even syllables can be utilized to strengthen your bond with Him and reach a level of peace both in body and mind. There is the ancient mantra, *Om* or *Rama*. There is the *Maha-mantra:*

Hare Rama, Hare Rama,
Rama, Rama, Hare, Hare;
Hare Krishna, Hare Krishna,
Krishna, Krishna, Hare, Hare.

being: Love, clarity, wisdom, courage. You focus on the issue and, on the in-breath, you imagine breathing that energy into your being. Hold your breath for a slow count of four and feel the energy fill your being. Breathe it in, hold it and let it fill your being, then emanate it outward with the out-breath. In this meditation we will be using colors, so breathe the color in, hold it and let it fill your being and then breathe it out and feel that color emanating from your being.

First Chakra

Draw the beam of white light down to the base of the spine. Hold this light in your First Chakra and visualize it turning a deep red. Hold your breath and focus on the physical nature of your senses. Feel yourself become passionate, strong, physical, and filled with courageous energy. As you breathe out, emanate the color red and feel its strength. Do this a few cycles until you enter into the feeling of the First Chakra.

Second Chakra

Again breathe the beam of white light to the base of your spine. Follow the energy up to the next chakra, located just above the pubic ridge. Visualize the energy becoming a deep orange color. While you bathe in this color, allow yourself to feel a sense of vitality and vigor. Recognize yourself as magnetic and know that you can attract to you all you need. Feel your sensuality awaken as your five senses come alive and, as you breathe out, send this magnetic, joyous energy out into the world.

Third Chakra

First, bring the beam of white light down to the base of your spine. Then, let it continue its upward journey to the area two-to-three inches above your navel, known as the solar plexus. Visualize the color changing to a brilliant yellow. Know yourself as a person endowed with independent choice in the expression of your will. Feel the clarity of your personal power, feel it firmly rooted in the values and convictions that you believe in. Feel yourself enter into a sense of total independence and breathe this clarity into the world.

Fourth Chakra

Bring the white light to the root chakra and let it move up to the area of the heart and visualize a rich forest-green color emanating from the heart. As you surround yourself with this refreshing ray, realize you are a totally loving, accepting person. Feel the abundance of life and know there is plenty of everything for everybody. Awaken to your generosity and share your heart with the world. Know that you can make decisions from your heart that will unite both your personal and spiritual needs.

Fifth Chakra

Bring the white ray to the base of your being and let it rise upward to your throat and immerse yourself in a sky-blue light. Let your thoughts be as boundless as the sky; allow your imagination to carry your vision to endless reaches of awareness. Awaken to your ability to view the world creatively and your capacity to express your true self. Awaken to your authentic self, liberated from cultural conditioning.

within, produce healing with soothing vibrations, so that we attain a level of experience that is deeper than mere thought.

Naam smaran, mantra japa, kirtan and *dhyana* are the very foundation of *abhyasa*. Together, they assuage the agitated mind and cleanse it of all impurities, leaving us calm and composed to enter into meditation.

PRACTICAL TIPS

» In meditation, the mantra is heard internally, not repeated aloud or heard externally.

» As the mantra is repeated internally, you will find that the mind becomes quieter and less distracted. Thoughts do arise, but it is possible to guide the mind back to its point of focus by concentrating on the mantra.

» Do not engage in conflict with your mind. Instead you should watch, observe and witness passing thoughts with detachment; allow them to pass and bring your mind back to the mantra gently, patiently and without any stress or strain. Any other reaction will only drain your mental energy.

» Do not attempt to drive away or suppress any thoughts. Just accept their presence without judgement and without intensifying them any further.

» Some mantras can be synchronized with your breathing – *So-Hum, Ra-Ma* or *O–M*. But not all mantras work in that manner. The goal of concentration is not to focus on the breathing

Heaven and Earth Meditation

SIT IN A comfortable meditation posture. Any posture that the spine is straight: lotus posture, in a chair, against a wall, or even lying down. Center yourself by focusing on your breath. Notice the in-breath and the out-breath. Notice the subtle rising in your being on the in-breath. Notice the subtle falling in of your being on the out-breath. Notice the changing of the breaths. See if you can even become aware of the sound of the subtle click in-between breaths. Ah, *center.*

Now practice playing the scales of your chakra system by focusing on each one in turn. Start with the First Chakra. Feel it by drawing your attention to it and see the color red and feel the attributes connected to this center. Move up through each of the chakras in succession by focusing on the appropriate colors (red, orange, yellow, green, blue, indigo, violet) and attributes. Then move back down the chakras from the Crown to the Root Chakra. Do this a few times, like playing the scales on a piano.

Next, imagine your spine extending down through the floor and into the earth. See roots growing out of the base of this extended spine, deep into the earth. See these roots entangling with the roots of the great trees and draw this

"The basis of spiritual life is the mantra, which vibrates with the energy of cosmic sound and which is a vehicle for spiritual transcendence. Mantra japa is considered to be the foremost sadhana in the Kali Yuga. When the mantra is imparted, it is registered on the atman, or soul. Through mantra repetition the gross mind becomes more and more subtle and refined. Mantra is used to create a state of harmony between external and internal life and unfold the psychic personality. Repetition of the mantra also gives relaxation, tranquillity and equipoise. A mantra can be obtained in three ways. It can be revealed to psychic people, it can manifest itself in a dream, or it can be received from a Guru."

– Swami Vibhuti Saraswati

The Tradition of *Japa* and Hindu *Bhakti*

Kabir man nirmal bhayo jaise Ganga neer
Peechhey peechhey Hari phirey kahat Kabir Kabir!

Kabir's mind has become as pure as the waters of the Ganga; and now, the Lord keeps following him, chanting Kabir, Kabir!

– Sant Kabir
(Indian Mystic poet and saint)

Our scriptures expound: *mananat trayate iti mantrah,* which means that a mantra is that which is chanted or thought of repeatedly, so as to liberate us from the cycle of birth and death.

Japa is the constant chanting of a mantra or the Name Divine. It is important to chant with concentration, devotion and deep faith. This form of dedicated repetition has a cleansing, purifying effect on our *antah karna* or inner instrument. Therefore, Kabir tells us that the *naam japa* made his heart so pure that the Lord started chanting his name and following him! In other words, *japa* had brought him close to divinity, to his true self!

Chakra	Drive	Core Issue	Perspective
1	*survival*	find place on earth	animal instinct; separate sense of self
2	*pleasure*	sensuality/sexuality	emotional self
3	*power*	will power; initiate activities and set boundaries	principles; what you stand for
4	*love*	open heart to all; non-competitive	cooperation
5	*creativity*	speak your truth	unique world-view beyond cultural conditioning
6	*transcendence*	be an inspiration to others	transcend polarities insightful
7	*spirituality*	connecting with Divine intent	seeing through the eyes of the Divine

Level of Consciousness	Unbalanced	Task
safety; connection to body and earth	insecurity	to be fully in the body
awareness of magnetic energy	hedonistic/ indulgent	to enjoy life
looking for opportunities for assertion of will	power conflicts	learn to choose wisely
being at peace	bleeding heart	joy
detach and observe without bias, then synthesize varying views	inadequacy or insensitivity	to be authentic
intuitive inner guidance from aligning with larger reality	spacing out; illusions	to be able to direct imagination
experiencing all of life as spiritual	"shopping list" mentality	surrender

ask my friends, "If while praying, we can think of worldly matters, why can't we think of God when we are attending to worldly matters?"

Scholars and experts classify mantras into three distinct types:

- *Saguna* mantras (those mantras addressed to God 'with form or attribute'): Many of them address a specific deity or aspect of the Divine, such as Lord Krishna, Lord Rama, Lord Shiva or Devi. e.g. *Om Namo Bhagavate Vasudevaya*
- *Nirguna* mantras ('without form or attribute') are based on the formless Divine. eg. *Om* and *So ham* ('I am He')
- *Bija* (seed) mantras are single-syllable sounds, whose verbal meaning is not available to us without initiation. They work through the power and energy of sound vibrations and are closely related to the chakras (energy centres within the body).

Japa is also of three types: chanted aloud, whispered in a low voice or uttered in the silence of the heart. Whichever form of *japa* we practice, the benefits we reap will be many: peace of mind, tranquility, increased concentration, positive energy levels and freedom from fear and anxiety.

I am sure that my readers are too intelligent to believe that such benefits can accrue from mechanical repetition alone! Faith and devotion are the magical ingredients that bestow power on any mantra or sloka.

Without these, we might as well be like the octogenarian Sanskrit pandit who was trying to memorize the rules of grammar, prompting Adi Shankara to compose his immortal hymn – *Bhaja Govindam:*

References and Suggested Reading

Bach, Richard. *Illusions.* New York, NY: Dell, 1977.

Barks, Coleman. *The Essential Rumi.* San Francisco, CA: Harper, 1995.

Blum, Ralph. *The Book of Runes.* New York, NY: St. Martins Press, 1982.

Brennan, Barbara. *Hands Of Light.* New York, NY: Bantam Books, 1988.

Bridges, Carol. *The Medicine Woman Inner Guidebook.* Nashville, IN: Earth Nation Publishing, 1987.

Carey, Ken. *Return Of The Bird Tribes.* San Francisco, CA: HarperCollins, 1988.

Chödrön, Pema. *When Things Fall Apart.* Boston, MA: Shambhala Publications, 1997.

———. *Start Where You Are.* Boston, MA: Shambhala Publications, 1994.

Coelho, Paulo. *The Alchemist.* San Francisco, CA: Harper, 1993.

in exploring what is possible for a human being. Learning Sanskrit is an opportunity to learn for ourselves what the rishis discovered long ago. Most importantly, when approached as a sacred language, it makes us happy."

Question: *What is the significance of a mantra?*
Answer: Every word has power; some words have less, others have more. A mantra is a word or a combination of words which have great power. If you continuously recite a mantra, you release tremendous spiritual energy which, among other things, helps you focus your wandering mind. The mind, as we know, has a tendency to keep on wandering all the time. And as the mind wanders, we wander with the mind. This wandering is the root cause of our unhappiness. If the mind is still or focused, we grow in peace of mind, which is the secret to true happiness.

Normally, the rays of the sun do not have the power to burn. But if a number of rays are brought to focus at one point, fire can be produced. Likewise, if the mind can be concentrated on one word, one idea or one set of powerful words, tremendous power is released.

Question: *Why should I get a* Guru *mantra?*
Answer: You should not think of getting a *Guru* mantra until you have the urge to do so without any shadow of a doubt. If the question arises in your mind, "Why should I ... ?" well, you should not. You should not ask for a *Guru* mantra because someone told you to.

Question: *Why are there so many mantras?*
Answer: A friend said to me, "India is a country that has specialized in spirituality; then why do we have so few mantras?"

It is all a matter of perspective!

The Power of the *Guru* Mantra

Dhyaana moolam gurur murthih
Poojaa moolam gurur padam
Mantra moolam gurur vakyam
Moksha moolam gurur kripa...

The word *diksha* is derived from the Sanskrit root *diksh*, which means 'to dedicate oneself'. Some scholars feel that it is derived from a combination of *diksh* (to consecrate, dedicate) and *daksh* (to grow, to expand or to become strong). We can, therefore, take *diksha* to mean 'expanding one's consciousness through complete dedication'.

Traditionally, *diksha* has been associated with the process of initiation at the Guru's hands. It is a process of both giving and receiving: we give our dedication, we offer our mind and soul to the Guru and, in turn, we receive the Guru's blessing to set out on the path of spiritual awakening. *Diksha* also means 'to see'; initiation at the hands of the Guru enables us to perceive our goal, our destination, more clearly. The Guru's blessing lights up the path before us, so that we can make progress towards spiritual growth.

As I mentioned earlier, we translate *diksha* as 'initiation'. This word also has rich and significant connotations in the

Index

rather than self-administer drugs based on our limited knowledge of medicine. So it is with our Guru, who is our spiritual healer, the physician of the soul. He knows what is best suited for our healing and spiritual welfare.

The *Guru* mantra, or the Name recommended by the Guru, has its own intrinsic value and energy as a *shabda*. More significantly, however, it carries with it the blessings and grace of the Guru, multiplying its powers manifold. Therefore, the *Guru* mantra is a combination of sacred sounds, high energy waves, healing vibrations and the transformative power of the Guru's special grace and compassion for us. Needless to say, this will actively enhance our spiritual progress.

Many of us can also vouch that our faith in the Guru, and the abundant love and devotion we have for him, also enhances the power and efficacy of the Name or the mantra that has been given to us. We can perceive this enhancement, when we recite and repeat it with greater faith and intensity than other prayers or slokas. When the faith and strong intent associated with the Guru *bhakti* are brought to bear on an already efficacious Name, we reap rich, spiritual rewards.

The *Guru* mantra also has this blessing – the Name bestowed by the Guru for us to chant, has no traces of egotistic achievement or ambition; we recite and repeat it with utter humility and deep gratitude for the Guru's grace. Elimination of the self and the ego, therefore, enhances the power of the Name.

Let me add a note of caution to aspirants who are setting out on the spiritual path. The name recommended to us by the Guru need not necessarily indicate initiation or official recognition of our status as a chosen disciple. I am afraid the term 'initiation' is bandied about today by many

The Value of the *Guru* Mantra

There was a devout young man who served his Guru with great faith and devotion. When the Guru felt he had evolved enough to tread the spiritual path on his own, he was called to present himself before the Guru. The Guru gave him a personal mantra and said to him, "This is a secret known to very few and I have bestowed it upon you. Please carry these sacred words within your heart. Take care not to divulge it to anyone – for it is very precious."

The disciple began to practice mantra *japa* with great sincerity and reverence. As he continued to recite it silently, the mantra was absorbed into his deepest consciousness.

One day, after a sacred dip in the river, the disciple passed by a few men who had just taken their bath. To his amazement, he heard them uttering the very same mantra aloud, as they smeared holy ash across their foreheads and prepared for the commencement of their morning rituals.

How can this be, the disciple thought to himself, my master told me to guard the secret mantra with my life and here, these men are repeating it aloud as as though it were a part of their daily routine… Could I have been mistaken… ?

When doubt enters the heart, who but the Guru can

resolve it? He went straight to his Guru and placed his problem at the holy one's feet.

The Guru heard him out patiently. Then he took a sizeable glossy stone from his pouch and gave it to the disciple. "Take it to the bazaar and show it to people you know," the Guru said to him. "Ask them what they think it is and what use they would put it to."

The disciple took the stone and said he would do as the Guru had asked. "Only remember, on no account must you give the stone away to anyone," the Guru added. "It must be brought back here without fail."

The disciple set out to complete the task. The first person he met in the bazaar was an old woman who sold vegetables to him on a daily basis.

"Take a look at this stone, *chachi*," he said showing her the glossy object. "What do you think it is?"

The old woman took it in her hand and peered closely at it.

"Looks like a piece of white marble," she said, handing it back to him.

"What would you do with it if it were yours?" the man enquired.

"You know *beta*, I need a 50 gram weight for my scales," the old lady said. "I could use this stone as a substitute for the missing weight."

The man took the stone and proceeded to the shop of his friend, a moneylender. The same questions were posed to him as well. The moneylender thought that the stone was an uncut semi-precious mineral, and said that he would use it as an unusual kind of paperweight.

Ganapati Mantra

Om Gan Ganapataye Namah

Lord Ganapati or Ganesha as He is known, is perhaps the most dearly beloved of Hindu deities. No prayer, ritual, pooja, indeed not even the daily routine activities of a pious Hindu household begin without invoking His name, for He grants all that is good and beneficial and takes away anything that might be detrimental to our good. He is worshipped as Vigneshwara – the One who removes all obstacles. He is the God of Power, Wisdom and Goodness.

Lord Ganapati is depicted as an elephant-headed deity riding a mouse – a form described by an ignorant few as being 'bizarre' or 'grotesque'. All we can say in condonation of such offensive remarks is that the people who utter them have not understood the symbolic significance of Hindu deities. The elephant-headed God, who has a mouse as his *vaahan* or vehicle, actually symbolizes Strength and Humility, Power sans Ego. Also remember that He symbolizes true wisdom. Our scriptures tell us: *Vidya dadati vinayam* – true wisdom and knowledge carry the hallmark of humility! This rare combination of strength and humility, power and sweet nature, wisdom and egolessness is what makes Lord

Om gananam tva ganapatim havamahe kavim
kavinamupamasravastamam
jyeshtaraajam brahmanam brahmanaspata aa nah
srnvannutibhissida saadanam
Mahaaganapathaye namah

> May we worship Lord Ganapati, the Protector of Noble People, the best Poet, the Most Honourable, the Greatest Ruler and the Treasure of all knowledge. O Ganapati, please listen to us and take your seat in our hearts.

One of the most well-known prayers to Lord Ganapati is the *Shri Ganapati Atharvashirsha,* which is to be found in the *Atharva Veda.* This text is considered to be the most important Vedic text on Lord Ganapati. It is regarded as a very powerful and efficacious stotra, especially in the state of Maharashtra, where entire communities and groups offer it as a collective public prayer.

Atharva means 'firm, stable and unwavering' – what we call one-pointedness of purpose. *Shirsha* means 'intellect'. The *Atarvashirsha* signifies that by disciplining and controlling the unsteady and wandering mind, our intellect and its efforts can be directed towards liberation or self-realization.

Most devotees of Lord Ganapati worship Him with the utterance of this simple mantra – *Om Gan Ganapataye Namah.* In this mantra, which begins with the *Moola* mantra-*Om,* we start with the *pranava shabda,* which is the pure consciousness of the Supreme. This is followed by a simple offering of devotion through salutations and prostrations to Lord Ganapati. Uttering this mantra will produce energy vibrations, which will remove all inner *kleshas* (anxieties and fears) and outer obstacles from our path.

The *Ganesha Gayatri* is also an ancient Vedic prayer which can be recited by the devout:

Ekadantaya Vidmahe Vakratundaya Dheemahi Tanno
Danti Prachodayat

We devote our thoughts to the One-Tusked Lord
We meditate upon Him who has a Curved trunk
May the tusked one guide us to the right path.

Children may be taught to recite this simple but beautiful and very effective sloka:

Vakratunda Mahakaaya
Suryakoti Samaprabha
Nirvighnam Kuru Mey Deva
Sarva Kaaryeshu Sarvada

O, Lord with the curved trunk and mighty body, who has the magnificence of a million suns, I pray to you, O Lord, to remove the obstacles from all the actions I intend to perform.

Mantras

TOOLS *for the* MIND

JP VASWANI

JAICO PUBLISHING HOUSE
Ahmedabad Bangalore Chennai
Delhi Hyderabad Kolkata Mumbai

back, come back at once! I can't manage this idol... I am going to put it down this minute!"

"Wait, wait please! For God's sake don't put it down," Ravana replied. "I will be with you in a moment!"

But by the time he had gotten out of the water, grabbed his clothes and came rushing back to the boy, the little lad had put the idol down, nullifying years and years of Ravana's *tapasya* and penance! Ravana stared daggers at the lad, who looked back at the rakshasa with complete innocence as if to say, "What did you expect me to do? It was too much for me!" In his anger and frustration, the heartless demon king actually boxed the little lad's ears, but the deed was done and the boon was lost! As for Lord Ganesha, sweet-natured as he was, he did not retaliate or hit back. He just continued looking at the demon king sweetly with complete innocence!

To this day, it is said that the *Atma Linga* at Gokarna is slightly bent where Ravana desperately tried to grab it from the ground, and the idol of Lord Ganesha also enshrined there, carries a scar on the forehead and a bent ear. This *stala purana* is narrated to us, so that we may remember that it is not for us to hit back at those who attack us: we must leave it to God to take care of us. The mighty and the powerful of this earth may bully us, but there is One who is more powerful, more intelligent than they!

POSITIVE VISUALIZATION

He is the Lord of auspicious beginnings and He blesses our efforts with successful endings.

As you prepare to begin the chanting, bring Lord Ganesha's radiant, auspicious form into your mind. As you

Contents

FREQUENTLY ASKED QUESTIONS (FAQS)

Question: *I am an American and am unable to pronounce the words of the mantra correctly. How important is the right pronunciation of the mantra?*
Answer: Right pronunciation of the mantra is very important. More important, however, is the spirit of love and devotion with which the mantra is chanted. Repeat the chant of the mantra with devotion as you work on improving the pronunciation. You will soon perfect it.

Question: *Does uttering the mantra help even if one does not understand its meaning? Is mechanical utterance alone effective?*
Answer: There are mantras that have no meaning at all. The mantra should be repeated with devotion as this will release the power which will help you in your spiritual quest.

Question: *Can I listen to a CD of the mantra instead of chanting it?*
Answer: The mantra should be chanted orally as far as possible. It is only when you utter it that you can fill it with the love and devotion of your heart.

Question: *I have heard that mantras generate powerful energy waves. Is this true?*
Answer: Yes, it is true!

The *Maha* Mantra

Hare Rama Hare Rama Rama Rama Hare Hare
Hare Krishna Hare Krishna Krishna Krishna
Hare Hare!

Of all the mantras known and recited by Hindus, this is perhaps the most loved, most sung and most chanted in public or private forms of prayer.

How and why did it come to be known as the *maha* mantra?

In the ancient scripture the *Brahmanda Purana,* Rishi Suta prays to the sage Veda Vyasa, asking him to expound the glories of the *Hari* mantra. This is the response he receives:

"The embodied soul who accepts this mantra will become filled with transcendence and by accepting it, even a drunkard will attain all perfections. I will recite this mantra to you, for you are a swan-like *mahabhagavata.*

Hare Krishna Hare Krishna Krishna Krishna Hare Hare, Hare Rama Hare Rama Rama Rama Hare Hare.

These sixteen names can destroy the sins of the three worlds, and nothing higher than them is to be found in all the *Vedas.*"

words of Francis Thompson, the English poet and ascetic, He is 'the Hound of Heaven'.

This beautiful relationship begins with a link that you can easily create by simply thinking of the Lord, taking His name into your heart and consciousness and chanting your favourite sloka or mantra repeatedly. For what is a mantra, but a specially charged set of words and sounds that form an expression of your devotion and faith? As you continue chanting it, the mantra acquires the power to make this love and devotion stronger and stronger. It effectively becomes your permanent link with the Divine!

Choose your favourite mantra – one that appeals to you and suits your need. Having chosen one, make it your own by internalizing its energy, positive vibrations and vitalizing pulse. Chant it constantly until it becomes a part of your consciousness. Believe me, it will transform your life!

People tell me that they cannot step out of their homes without their mobile phones, that both their professional and private lives are tied up in their notepads and laptops. Others even claim that they cannot survive without their credit cards. *Connectivity* is the byword of this age! I respect the need to stay connected through the use of these gadgets and devices, but I urge you to remember that there is one important connection that should never be overlooked – your link with your Creator, your Father. This must remain your ultimate goal beyond the passing affairs of this world.

Japa yoga, repetition of the Name Divine, is the easiest sadhana that is available to us today. The power of the Name is sweeter than nectar and more auspicious than both good luck and good omens combined. This power has been concentrated into the great mantras that have been passed on to us from our ancient scriptures. We know that they were heard in states of elevated consciousness by realized souls and then handed down to us for our benefit. Is it not incumbent upon us to claim our birthright as the true inheritors of these treasures?

What are the benefits of chanting these sacred mantras? Though there are too many to enumerate, let me touch upon a few very briefly:

1. First and foremost, the rare and precious gift of peace of mind; calmness and tranquility; freedom from needless tension and anxiety.
2. The feeling of security in connecting with a power that is higher than us; the profound perspective that we hold a place in the vast cosmic order that is controlled like Divine clockwork.
3. The power to conquer negative thinking and lower sense-desires.
4. The generation of new spiritual energy that can neutralize past samskaras and clear the mind of accumulated *vaasanas,* which drag us down through the endless cycle of birth-death-rebirth.
5. Constant chanting and remembrance of a mantra takes you closer to God – a feeling that cannot be described in words, it must be experienced!
6. Each mantra, chanted with absolute devotion and faith, helps us achieve the fourfold goal of this human life – *dharma, artha, kama and moksha.*

Naam gaao! Naam gaao! is the call of our saints and Gurus. The Lord Himself recommends *Japa* as His chosen form of worship. Therefore in this book, I have brought together a few familiar and well-known mantras along with considered reflections on each.

"In this age there is no use in meditation, sacrifice and temple worship. Simply by chanting the holy name of Krishna – Hare Krishna, Hare Krishna, Krishna Krishna, Hare Hare/Hare Rama, Hare Rama, Rama Rama, Hare Hare – one can achieve perfect self-realization."

(*Vishnu Purana* 6.2.17)

"The self-realization which was achieved in the Satya millennium by meditation, in the Treta millennium by the performance of different sacrifices, and in the Dvapara millennium by worship of Lord Krishna [as the Deity in the temple], can be achieved in the age of Kali simply by chanting the holy names, Hare Krishna, Hare Rama."

(*Srimad Bhagavatam* 12.3.52)

"Living beings who are entangled in the complicated meshes of birth and death can be freed immediately, by even unconsciously chanting the holy name of Krishna, which is feared by fear personified."

(*Srimad Bhagavatam* 1.1.14)

"When instructing King Parikshit, the great sage Sri Shukadeva said, 'O King, constant chanting of the holy name of the Lord after the ways of the great authorities is the doubtless and fearless way of success for all, including those who are free from all material desires, those who are desirous of all material enjoyment, and also those who are self-satisfied by dint of transcendental knowledge. What is the value of a prolonged life which, inexperienced by years in this world? Better a moment

The Value of Mantras

A mantra is a sacred utterance that is characteristically associated with India's great, ancient scriptures – the *Vedas,* which are a collection of hymns and sacred utterances that have survived for millennia through oral transmission. Therefore, a mantra is intrinsically connected to sound; its special powers are as much in the depth of its meaning as in the vibrations produced by chanting. Many people believe that a mantra has transformative powers, which can bring about spiritual rejuvenation. Hinduism believes that a mantra is a sacred verbal formula repeated in prayer, meditation or incantation. An invocation of God or a verse from an ancient scripture, are both common examples of mantras. Many mantras associated with the Hindu faith are normally in Sanskrit. They have become such an integral part of sacred rites and rituals that those who utter them, as well as those who hear them, are esteemed as beneficiaries of a mantra's special vibrations and spiritual energy.

The word mantra contains two syllables – *man,* which means 'to think' (also as in *manas* or mind) and the suffix *tra,* which means 'tool'. A loose translation of the term mantra would be an 'instrument of thought'. It must be emphasized however, that a mantra does not have a fixed or definite meaning. There are numerous ways to interpret it. In fact, it would be as futile to try and explain this mantra to you, as it would be to try and capture the essence of the beauty and fragrance of an Indian rose! "Five red petals, soft pollen, circular overlapping arrangement of outer petals… " – this description is nowhere near capturing the beauty of the rose, is it? So, too, with the *maha* mantra: chant it, recite it with others, repeat it in the silence of your heart – and you will discover its power and beauty.

If we were to look at this mantra, we would see that it is made up of 16 words, but just three words are actually repeated again and again *Hare, Rama* and *Krishna,* or *Hare, Krishna* and *Rama* if you prefer the order in which the devotees of the Krishna Consciousness repeat it. I do not need to be a scholar or a philosopher to tell you that Rama and Krishna are the Divine Names taken on by Lord Vishnu in His Seventh and Ninth incarnations. Lord Rama and Lord Krishna are perhaps closer to us than all the other incarnations. But, as Jiva Goswami, Tulsidas, Vallabha Acharya and Narsi Mehta discovered, Lord Rama and Lord Krishna are One – the Supreme Lord of the Universe.

It would be inappropriate in this context to ask what's in a name. It is because millions and millions of devout Hindus have been uttering these Names for thousands and thousands of years, that the names of Rama and Krishna have acquired the power and energy that they offer us. The love, devotion, longing and spiritual intensity with which our people have uttered these Names, have added to their already potent power and made them vibrate with such resonance, that we are thrilled at the very sound of their utterance and feel elevated to a state of absolute faith and peaceful surrender!

The word *Hare* is traced by some people to its root

form *Haran,* which means to 'take away' or 'to end'. So, when we chant *Hare Krishna,* we are asking God to take away our sorrows, sufferings, misfortunes, as well as our negative karmas and our weaknesses. Depending on the type of individual we happen to be, we can ask for material abundance and worldly success through this mantra, or we can ask the Lord to give us the ultimate gift that he alone can give – the gift of Liberation from the cycle of birth and death. Therefore, the *maha* mantra is actually a prayer to God to take away all our sorrows and pains (on whichever level of consciousness we dwell) and to replace them with pure peace and bliss!

Other mantras include *Om Namoh Bhagavate Vaasudevaaya, Om Namah Shivaaya, Om Sri Rama, Jaya Rama, Jaya, Jaya, Rama, Rama Krishna Hari, Satnaam, Waahguru* and *Om Mani Padme Hum.* Even the simple repetition of names or phrases from other faiths can be a mantra: 'Lord Jesus Christ, have mercy on me', Jehovah, Ya Allah and Ahura Mazda. The list is endless.

Mantras – an Aid to Meditation

Many meditative techniques assimilate mantras. An extremely important attribute we must remember, is that a mantra should be heard internally, not externally.

As we have seen, in its strictest form, a mantra is not an expression with meaning; it is a sound, a *shabda* with its own distinctive vibrations. Undoubtedly, if we utter the sacred Name aloud, the sound creates its own waves. But when mantras vibrate in silence, within us, they have an exceedingly agreeable effect on our being. In fact, according to Hindu tradition, the ancient sages who sat in deep lifelong meditation, felt these vibrations in the silence within their souls. The sounds they heard – *shruti* – have become the mantras we use today.

These days, we attach meaning and value only to uttered words; the eloquence of silence is lost to most of us. Therefore, it takes practice to appreciate and absorb the vibrations that a mantra produces. Rather than looking for just any meaning at all, we must learn to *experience* the vibrations at a profound level.

A whole book could be written on the fascinating subject of the interrelation between mantras and meditation. It suffices to say, however, that mantras which are heard from herself that her conquest of the saint would definitely be accomplished that night. But when night came, she found that she could not lure the saint from his chanting and that at night she was irresistibly drawn, as if by magic, to the Divine vibrations of the chanting!

On the third night, she came early to the saint's cottage, so that she could listen to the chanting from the beginning. And the mere listening of the *maha* mantra transformed her completely. She thought to herself, "Men have told me that I am the most beautiful form they have ever beheld. But the humble saint here must have attained something far more beautiful than myself. This must be the reason why he won't even so much as look at me! Otherwise, he would have fallen into the trap of my beauty just as a moth flies into a flame. Let me also attain the Beauty of all beauties which has intoxicated this saint."

At the dawn of the fourth day, she fell at the feet of *Bhakta* Haridas and asked to be accepted as his disciple. She gave all her wealth to the poor and the needy in return for a *tulsi mala* from the saint, and devoted the rest of her life to chanting the Name Divine!

POSITIVE VISUALIZATION

As you sit down to chant the *maha* mantra, start by repeating it softly, melodiously and rhythmically. Notice that it blends beautifully with your thoughts and each breath you take. Of all the mantras, it is the easiest, the sweetest and the most effortless to recite!

Once you have enjoyed the pleasurable chanting and the peace it spontaneously brings with it, begin to visualize Lord Rama.

process. If you do, you will only create a distraction and disrupt the breathing process.

- Remember, mantras cannot simply be read and learnt from books; it is much more effective for a qualified yoga teacher to give his students a personal mantra suited to their level of experience.
- If you have not received a mantra, you can meditate with one that is enshrined in the soul of India – *Om* (also pronounced as 'aum') or the sacred name, *Rama*.

Many people today are turning to meditation to reduce the effects of stress and anxiety, to grow in awareness and to improve their health or emotional stability. It is through effective meditation that they achieve the results they are looking for. However, it must not be forgotten that the true goal of meditation is God. Meditation should aim at detaching the heart from all that is not related to God – the sole purpose should be to build a communion with the Divine Being. Therefore, even in the midst of your daily work, pause for a moment and breathe out an aspiration such as, "I love You, God! I want to love You more and more! I want to love You more than anything in the world! I want to love You to distraction! Grant me pure love and devotion for Your Lotus Feet and so bless me that this world-bewitching maya may not lead me astray and make me, Blessed Master, an instrument of Thy help and healing in this world of suffering and pain!"

Where there is love, meditation becomes easy and natural.

FREQUENTLY ASKED QUESTIONS (FAQS)

Question: *The maha mantra is said to be the surest way to attain the realization of God in the present age. Does that mean it is more powerful than the* Guru *mantra?*
Answer: No mantra can be more powerful than the *Guru* mantra, provided it is given to you by a realized soul. Stick to the *Guru* mantra like a postage stamp and it will deliver you to your goal!

Question: *Can the chanting of a mantra reduce the adverse impact of the* Grahas?
Answer: Yes, mantras do possess the power to reduce the evil effects of a *graha.*

Question: *Can mantras mitigate our karmas?*
Answer: If a mantra is properly used, it will take you to a plane that transcends karma.

Question: *Which is the better of the two: to repeat the mantra verbally or to repeat the mantra silently within your heart?*
Answer: A mantra uttered in a whisper or within your heart is many times more powerful and efficacious than a mantra that is repeated loudly. However, this does not apply to mantras that are recited in a congregation.

The *Gayatri* Mantra

Om bhur bhuvah svah
tat-savitur varenyam
bhargo devasya dhimahi
dhiyo yo nah prachodayat

> Oh God, the Protector, the basis of all life, Who is self-existent, Who is free from all pains and Whose contact frees the soul from all troubles; Who pervades the Cosmos and sustains all, the Creator and Energizer of the whole Cosmos, the Giver of happiness, Who is worthy of acceptance; the most excellent, Who is Pure and the Purifier of all; let us embrace that very God, so that He may direct our mental faculties in the right direction.

Just as powerful and potent mantras from the scriptures have the energy to transform our lives, so too, we may say, that some of these mantras acquire far greater power and energy when they are chanted by the devout over thousands of years. The sacred *Gayatri* mantra is such a mantra, that is capable of heightening, elevating and ennobling our lives at all levels. Today, it is chanted by everyone: the young and the old, the rich and the poor, men and women alike; even foreigners and people belonging to other faiths believe in the efficacy and uplifting capacity of this mantra. Instead of

When we talk to *abhyasis* or regular practitioners, they will tell us that mantra *japa* brings the form of God before their mind's eye and establishes His beauteous vision in their hearts. Therefore, those who chant *Om Namo Narayana* behold the vision of Lord Hari and His form gradually gets imprinted into their consciousness. Similarly, chanting *Om Namah Shivaya* brings the form of Lord Shiva into their minds and hearts. Indeed, *naam japa* is the easiest and quickest way to God in this age of *Kali* in which we are destined to live.

As I have explained earlier, most of the sacred mantras of the Hindu faith have their origins in the *Vedas*. These are mostly expressed in the form of a two-line couplet or verse known as the sloka, which is unique to our ancient scriptures. By definition, a sloka is a grammatical/metrical form of verse and this is the metrical pattern of the *Vedas* and the *Puranas*. A sloka may also be a verse, phrase, proverb or hymn of praise, usually composed in a specified meter (a verse of two lines, each of sixteen syllables). The sloka is the primary form of verse in the Sanskrit epics: the *Mahabharata*, the *Ramayana* and the *Bhagavad Gita*, all of which are read, recited or chanted in silence as part of the devotional practices of the people in this country.

The regular and constant chanting of these mantras and slokas became a practice among the faithful during the rise and growth of the great *Bhakti* movement in India. Verses from the *Vedas*, as well as devotional chants of the Name Divine, became a part of *kirtan, naam japa, bhajans* and hymns, in which the devout participated as a group or engaged in congregational activity. Therefore, *japa* became an essential part of the Hindu spiritual tradition. So, when a mantra was repeated in this manner, it was called mantra *japa*; when the Name of the Lord was recited on its own, it became *naam japa.*

The Sanskrit word *japa,* is derived from the root word *jap,* which means 'to utter in a low voice, or repeat mentally'. Constant repetition of a chosen Name or mantra can even lead to a sense of identification with the object of meditation – the Supreme Lord. *Japa* calms the mind and aids concentration; it is said that after intense and continuous practice, the chanting continues in one's mind without conscious effort, even during work and sleep, as a kind of steadfast spiritual awareness. Ultimately, this may result in the state of *samadhi* or oneness with the Divine Self.

Japa inspires, awakens and enhances the practice of *bhakti yoga.* Through the mystic powers inherent in the Name or the mantra, there is a rise in Divine energy, grace and shakti. Like the purifying power of fire, *japa* also has the capacity to burn all the karmic residues of our past sins and negative karmas, leaving us in a state of higher consciousness that is close to true bliss or *sat chit ananda.*

Let me tell you, especially for the benefit of new aspirants who wish to tread the pilgrim path, we do not have to confine *japa* or repetition of the Divine Name to a special ritual bound by rules and regulations. As we become habituated to *japa,* it becomes such a natural part of our life, that it is no longer an activity restricted or exclusive to certain places and certain times. It comes as naturally to us as breathing and does not even interfere with our daily duties and activities. Whether you are driving, walking, cooking, cleaning or attending to your work, *japa* goes on in your mind, uninterrupted. This state of habitual *japa* can only be attained after long and sustained practice of intensive repetition. Therefore, I often *bhuloka,* the *pitru loka* and the *deva loka;* 2) the three worlds of the cosmos: earth, air and space; and 3) at a more subtle level, the microcosm of the human body, mind and spirit. The mantra proper which follows is a prayer:

tát savitúr várenyam
bhárgo devásya dhīmahi
dhíyo yó nah prachodáyāt

This is a prayer to the God Savitar, which may be translated as:

> May we attain that excellent glory of Savitar the God:
> So He may stimulate our prayers.

There are 24 syllables in this mantra. One thousand verses in Valmiki's *Ramayana* begin with each of these syllables, thus making the 24,000 verses of the sacred epic a glorious tribute to this sacred mantra that is truly beloved of our saints and sages!

The *Gayatri* is also unique in that it embodies the three attributes of devotion common to all Hindu mantras: the concepts of *stotra* (singing the praise and glory of God), *dhyaana* (meditation) and *praarthana* (prayer).

Gayantam Trayate iti Gayatri: *Gayatri* is that which protects those who sing it, so say our sages. The chanting of this mantra is especially beneficial at what are known as *sandhya* times of the day: sunrise, midday and sunset.

In Hindu rites, the *Gayatri* mantra is first taught to boys who undergo their *Upanayanam* or Sacred Thread Ceremony. The father of the boy, taking the position of his first Guru, whispers the mantra into his son's ear, thus initiating him into the daily ritual of chanting the mantra. Therefore, in

Worship Govinda, Chant Govinda, Adore Govinda, O fool!

When the appointed time of death arrives grammar rules surely will not save you.

Worship Govinda, Chant Govinda, Adore Govinda, O fool!

For there is no other way to cross the life's ocean except lovingly remembering the holy names of God!

FREQUENTLY ASKED QUESTIONS (FAQS)

Question: *Why are many of our mantras and slokas in Sanskrit?*

Answer: Vyaas Houston, the founder of the American Sanskrit Institute, tells us that Sanskrit is "the language of the mantra, words of power subtly attuned to the unseen harmonies of the matrix of creation."

He adds: "The extraordinary thing about Sanskrit is that it offers direct accessibility to anyone to that elevated plane, where the two, mathematics and music, brain and heart, analytical and intuitive, scientific and spiritual, become one. This is fertile ground for revelation.

"Sanskrit is like a crystalline river, flowing with tremendous force to the ocean of our eternal, all pervading being. The vibrational purity and resonating power of Sanskrit, as well as the meanings conveyed in its awesome body of sacred literature, is an opera on a cosmic scale that you can sing with your whole heart and being.

"Sanskrit is the living heritage of great rishis, the enlightened ones who walked this earth thousands of years ago. It presents us with a compelling responsibility and a lifelong challenge, while it inspires us to remain fully engaged from all harm and bring God's grace upon all those who hear it or recite it. Its utterance is considered equal to the reading of the four *Vedas*. In it, we hear the Supreme Harmony of the cosmos and attain oneness with the self, which leads to the still centre within us to connect us directly with the Divine. I must also stress that most people who recite this mantra do not ask for material gifts or worldly power; they seek the highest awareness which may link them with the splendour and radiance of the Divine!

There is so much that has been written and said about the power and significance of this mantra – some of it complex, some of it profound and some of it esoteric and out of the grasp of the common man or woman. I am no scholar, I am just a seeker and pilgrim on the path. Therefore, I refrain from discussing the more abstruse versions of this profound mantra. I would urge all of you to make this mantra your own and chant it aloud or softly when you can. Chant it within the silence of your heart constantly, so that it becomes one with you, one with the breath of your being.

Sage Vishwamitra and the *Gayatri* Mantra

All of us are familiar with the story of Sage Vishwamitra, one of the great sages who played a leading role in the *Ramayana* as a mentor to Lord Rama. He was also instrumental in arranging Lord Rama's marriage to the Goddess Sita.

The real story of Sage Vishwamitra begins under very different circumstances. He was actually a great Kshatriya warrior and king, called Kaushika. Marching with his famished army across a deserted and lonely region, King Kaushika received hospitality at the humble *kutiya* of Sage Vashishta. To his utter amazement, not only did the sage offer a banquet for him and his sons but simultaneously arranged for thousands of his footsoldiers to be fed as well. Amazed by this feat, King Kaushika demanded to know how an indigent ascetic living in a lonely ashram could arrange for such a feast at such short notice. That is when he came to know of the heavenly calf Nandini, daughter of the Divine wish-fulfilling cow, Kamadhenu. Nandini had been gifted to Sage Vasishta by the gods, so that he could concentrate on his *yajnas* and *tapasya* without undue worldly worries. But Kaushika failed to perceive the significance of the wish-fulfilling calf being left with an ascetic; he felt that he had more claim to such a

English language: to begin, to set going, to originate or to admit a new person through formal rites. *Diksha* works through several levels, starting with the formal, external ceremony or ritual that then extends to one's deepest level of consciousness. It involves the transmission of the Guru's grace, which can be bestowed upon the disciple in many ways, depending on his level of aspiration and attainment.

Formal and more subtle methods of initiation have been associated with all the ancient religions of the world. Later religions, like Christianity and Islam, also continued to practice it in some form or other.

A holy saint defines *diksha* as "the inner link between a Guru and his disciple which is formed through initiation, working as a transmitting link of spiritual flow, spiritual awareness and spiritual energy."

Although there are different forms of initiation practiced by different sects, the most well-known form of initiation is mantra *diksha.*

A mantra that we take from a book does not have the same significance and value as one that is received through the voice of a realized master – our Guru. Receiving a mantra from the mouth of the Guru is the sacred process of mantra *diksha,* as it is the significant beginning, the first step that an aspirant takes on the spiritual path. When the sacred mantra is uttered by the Guru, the disciple receives the sound of the mantra and as soon as it reaches the deepest level of his consciousness, he is then said to be initiated.

This initiation is of the utmost significance to all aspirants. In its truest and most profound form, it is not just an utterance that is passed on, but a spontaneous spiritual experience. Therefore, an ancient text tells us: "A mantra is not mastered even after repeating it a billion times, by a person who does not know the esoteric meaning of it, and has not experienced its awakening power." It is believed that these can only be transmitted by the Guru to those who are *fit* and *ready* to receive it.

Today, many people – men and women, young and old – are eager to receive mantra *diksha* from their spiritual masters. Genuine gurus, however, are very particular about each aspirant having attained a certain level of preparedness before a formal initiation is given.

Our scriptures also tell us that an aspirant who approaches the Guru for mantra *diksha,* should have certain qualifications. After all, it is futile to sow seeds without preparing the soil; unless the mind is pure and ready, mantras cannot take root. The best way to prepare the mind is through good conduct, sincerity, devotion, humility and intense yearning. If one seeks mantra *diksha* with these qualities, his efforts will be greatly rewarded.

The term Guru mantra, in most cases, refers to a particular name of the Lord, rather than a prayer or an actual mantra that has been given to us by our Guru.

The efficacy of a mantra bestowed upon us by the Guru lies in his intuitive wisdom. The Guru is aware of our spiritual need and the level of our spiritual growth. He can then accordingly choose the right Name or *naama* to assist our progress to eventual liberation. We are not in any condition to understand our own needs in this regard: only the Guru is capable of offering this guidance.

Doctors often warn us against the heedless practice of self-medication. They insist that we consult a medical practitioner and take the prescription based on his diagnosis,

POSITIVE VISUALIZATION

Before you begin chanting, close your eyes and offer your devotion to *Gayatri* as the *Vedamata* – the personification of wisdom, light and life-giving energy.

Begin chanting the mantra in silence, dwelling on the significance of each sound, each word and each line. Feel the vibrations the mantra creates within you.

As the chanting continues, feel yourself become a part of this vast cosmic order that has come into being through the Divine Will and is operating on Divine Energy. The sun, the moon, the stars and the planets are each in their proper spheres. The five elements are functioning according to their nature and purpose. The earth is revolving on its ordained orbit and everything in this vast universe moves according to the Divine Will.

Believe that you are a part, a tiny but essential part, of this vast cosmic plan! Feel the omnipotent, omniscient presence of the Divine Energy, the Supreme all-pervading *Brahman*, Who is animating, managing and controlling this entire universe! Feel the energy of the universe! God is not afar from you! He is within you, just as He is in all that is! You belong in the universe. You have your place and your existence has a purpose as does each star and planet in the heavens!

Feel that you are being blessed by the omnipresent, all pervasive, brilliant, pure energy of Divinity. Be aware that this mantra will protect you and give you the wisdom and correct thinking, so as to tread on the path of dharma, of righteousness!

Let the vibrations of pure Divine Energy envelop you as you continue chanting. Feel the light and the warmth ambitious aspirants, almost as if it were akin to a pass to attend a special event or admission to a new course obtained through influence! Many Gurus recommend short prayers, one-line or two-line scriptural verses or even positive, motivational quotes to purify our consciousness and cleanse us of negativity. Therefore, Spiritual masters recommend the chanting of the Name Divine in large groups, or special prayers to be recited by the congregation. All these are excellent aids to inner cleansing and purification. The *Guru* mantra itself is bestowed only upon those whom the Guru judges to be ready for initiation – those disciples inspired by the intense longing for liberation or *mumukshatwa*.

Whatever Name, mantra or short saying the Guru teaches us and urges us to repeat, becomes a powerful and potent healing influence on our lives! To reap its profound benefits, all we need is to simply repeat it with faith and constancy!

The repetition of the mantra bestowed upon you by your Guru, has great power and efficacy. Not only does it strengthen your faith and devotion, but it also purifies your mind, heart and soul. Our saints and sages tell us that *naam smaran* can absolve us of all sins and lead us on to salvation, but this is possible only when the mantra is uttered with perfect faith and reverence. The mantra that is heard within the heart is far more efficacious than the one uttered aloud.

The *Maha Mrityunjaya* Mantra

Om Trayambakam Yajamahe,
Sugandhim Pushtivardhanam;
Urva Rukamiva Bandhanaan,
Mrityor Mokshiye Maamritat.

We worship Shiva, The Three-Eyed (*trayambakam*) Lord (*yajamahe*);
Who is fragrant (*sugandhim*) and nourishes (*pushti*) and helps all beings grow (*vardhanam*).
Even as the ripened cucumber (*urvarukamiva*) is automatically liberated (*bandhanaan*) (by the intervention of the "farmer") from its bondage to the creeper when it fully ripens;
May He liberate us (*mokshiya*) from death (*mrityor*), for the sake of immortality (*maamritat*).

This great and powerful mantra, invoking Shiva as the Lord of death, is found in the *Rig Veda*. The word *mrityunjaya* means that which conquers death. We call it the *maha mrityunjaya* mantra, for it is indeed the Great Death-Conquering mantra.

Scholars also refer to this as the *mrita-sanjivini* mantra, because it is believed to have been given to Sage Shukracharya (the Guru of the asuras) as a life-restoring boon after he had completed an exhausting period of austerity. It is said that he hung from the branch of a tree, above a scorching fire that continuously burnt his skin for 20 long years. In this vein, I must add that the term *urvarukam,* translated above as a ripe cucumber, also has other meanings – pain, disease and physical suffering. Therefore, the mantra can also offer us protection against physical ailments, which we all fall victim to at some point in our lives.

The *Markandeya Purana* gives us a fascinating account of the effect of this mantra:

Sage Mrikandu and his wife Marudhvati were ardent devotees of Lord Shiva. Pleased with their devout life and austerities, Lord Shiva gave them His *darshan* and asked them to name a boon of their choice, which he would willingly grant to them.

The couple, being childless, asked the Lord to grant them a son.

Now began a *leela* of the Lord. "I grant you the boon of a son, as you desire," Lord Shiva said to them. "But you must make a choice: would you like to have a son who is dull and low in wisdom, but would live to be a 100 years old or would you like to have a distinguished, enlightened and evolved son, who will die at the age of 16?"

Without the least hesitation, the sage and his wife chose the second option – a wise and brilliant son, whose life would be very short. And thus, was born to them, Markandeya, – exemplary and noble in every way. He mastered the *Vedas* and the scriptures at a very early age and grew up to be a great Shiva *bhakta* like his father.

The parents who had watched him with great joy, blossom into a young yogi and *jnani,* began to dread the approach of his 16th birthday. Unaware of the early death which awaited

A little farther down was the shop frequented by the aspirant's wife. This shop sold artificial jewellery. When the jeweller saw the stone, he pronounced it to be an artificial diamond. "I would cut it up and use it to make jewels," he said.

The last stop was at the office of his cousin who was a gemmologist. The cousin took one look at the stone and said, "Who gave this to you? It is one of the largest diamonds I have ever seen!"

"A real diamond?" stammered the young man. "What would you do with it if it were yours?"

"It is of no use to me as it is," said the jeweller. "People just can't afford to buy a diamond of this size. It will have to be cut, polished and sold."

The disciple thanked him and took the stone back to the Guru. Faithfully, he repeated what he had heard from the people he met.

"I hope your doubt is resolved now," the Guru said to him. "The diamond is priceless in its present form, but nobody recognized this. Their only concern was to put it to a limited use in the light of their thinking and experience. Similarly, the mantra I gave you is a priceless treasure, others misuse it because they do not know its true value. You must realize its worth and guard it as a treasure."

Therefore, we are told in the *Guru Gita*:

Dhyaana moolam gurur murthih
Poojaa moolam gurur padam
Mantra moolam gurur vakyam
Moksha moolam gurur kripa...

The root of meditation is the Guru's form; the root of worship is the Guru's feet; the root of mantra is the Guru's word. The root of liberation is the Guru's grace.

FREQUENTLY ASKED QUESTIONS (FAQS)

Question: *I have two Gurus in my life, would it hasten my spiritual progress if I get two* Guru *mantras*?
Answer: As I have already said, it is better to concentrate on one word, one idea or one mantra. Therefore, having two *Guru* mantras will not hasten, but could in fact hinder your progress. It is the quality of the chant not the quantity of mantras that ultimately makes the difference.

Question: *Can I choose a mantra that appeals to me rather than asking my Guru for one?*
Answer: You can choose your own mantra, but just as getting a prescription from a doctor is always better than prescribing oneself medicine, it is always better to get a mantra from a truly spiritually evolved soul.

Question: *Does the* Guru *mantra help after death?*
Answer: Lord Krishna says in the *Gita,* that the effort you put in will never go in vain. Life is like a continuous stream – the strength or power you gather here will be helpful to you during your time on earth as well as in the great beyond.

Question: *I am unable to concentrate or meditate in silence on the mantra. Would it still be effective if I simply write it instead of uttering it?*
Answer: This is what we call *Likhit japa.* If on a particular day you are unable to concentrate on the mantra, you would do well to write it again and again.

Let me tell you right away that conquering death in this context does not mean living in this present physical body, in this present life of ours, for thousands and thousands of years! This mantra is certainly not the philosopher's stone referred to in legends of alchemy.

Death is the one unalterable verity of human life. It is a cliché to say that all that is born must die; yet that is the truth. He who is born has to die, but how many of us understand the meaning of death? What is death? What kind of experience brings down the curtain on the drama that is our life? If the truth must be told, many of us are superstitious about discussing death; we are frightened by the very word *death*. We shy away from the very thought of death.

Can you imagine a state of mind or an attitude in which we detach ourselves from this material existence, and cultivate the awareness that this perishable human body is simply worn as a garment while our true self is the immortal atman? If we can reach this level of awareness, if we can cultivate this sense of detachment from the physical and material plane of existence – then we can truly claim that we have conquered the fear of death!

We cannot avoid death, but we can certainly avoid this obsessive fear of death. It is said by the brave that each of us has but one life to live and, therefore, we can die but once. It is the cowardly who 'die' several times before death actually comes to them. If we are to come to terms with death, if we are to overcome this fear of death, we must get to know more about death.

Life is a mixture of both pleasant and unpleasant experiences. Death is the ultimate experience, which is why it is unique. I would add that it is also an extraordinary

Ganapati beloved of the rich and the poor, the mighty and the ordinary alike!

The problem with our present age is that the powerful and mighty lack compassion and wisdom, while the truly wise and intelligent lack the strength of will and power to exert their good influence. *Lambodara, Mahakaaya,* the enormous One as He is lovingly described, redresses this imbalance. Nowadays we all need *sanmati* or good thinking; the virtues of love, compassion, charity and patience need to be reinforced and strengthened; the weak need to be protected and their hands need to be strengthened; as for those who are already blessed with strength and power, they need the influence of *jnana* or true wisdom, which will enable them to channelize their energy and strength into constructive work. Therefore, Lord Ganesha is the One who can grant us exactly what we need: to address and neutralize our particular deficiencies and desires.

Lord Ganapati is actually the embodiment of an infinite and all-pervasive Divine energy. Although He is dearly loved by everyone, old and young, and approached without reservation, as one would a dear friend or elder sibling for invaluable help or guidance, He represents the vast and formless principle of Divine power.

It is Lord Ganapati who is invoked first in all *yajnas* and rites. It is His name that all Hindus repeat at the beginning of any form of worship. Indeed, the name of Lord Ganapati occurs right at the beginning of the *Rig Veda,* which is thought to be the most ancient among the scriptures. This *Veda* gives us the well-known mantra:

us away from this world to an astral sphere. In a Trappist monastery abroad, I saw written in bold letters the words, *Carpo Mori,* meaning 'Contemplate on Death'. Think of it everyday. "Death is sure to come, but fortunate is he who has made preparations for that day." These are the meaningful words of my master, Sadhu Vaswani. We have to prepare for death and when it comes, we must welcome it with open arms – for it takes us one step nearer to God.

Symbolically, this mantra may also be taken as a prayer to Lord Shiva to lead us to His abode – Kailash, which is the Mountain of Meditation. In other words, it is a prayer to avoid living in the darkness of ignorance, which is the equivalent of a spiritual death. As the *tryambaka* or Three-Eyed Lord, it is He who can lift the veils of maya to uncover our third eye so as to awaken us spiritually. This kind of awakening should naturally lead us to liberation or moksha. This is the goal of all human life. This is a state that must be sought after, not feared or avoided!

Therefore, we can say that this mantra is a prayer for enlightenment; its chanting can help us neutralize negative karma at the deepest level of the spirit. It is also a beneficial aid to the mental, emotional, and physical well-being of man.

The Story of the Merchant and His Parrot

There lived a wealthy merchant in the kingdom of Arabia. He had three daughters whom he loved dearly. He also had a clever parrot which he kept in a golden cage in his room. The parrot was his most prized possession, for it could speak wisely and well.

Once, the merchant had to travel to India to buy silks, spices and precious gems for his trade. He asked each of his daughters what they would like from India. Like all young girls, they demanded gold, jewels, silken robes and other valuable gifts.

"You shall have all that your heart desires," he assured them heartily. Then he turned to his pet parrot. "And what about you, dear creature?" he asked. "You are no less dear to me than my daughters. Tell me, what can I bring for you from the famed and historical land of Bharata?"

"There is something I want in particular from there," said the parrot. "I would like you to find a flock of parrots in India and ask them to answer just one question of mine: *How can I attain freedom?* Bring back their answer, for I have heard that even birds are wise in that ancient land."

Lord Ganesha and Ravana

Let me narrate to you a little-known story from our ancient books, relating to the *stala purana* (temple history) of the great pilgrimage centre, Gokarna, located on the west coast of India.

Ravana had undertaken a severe penance (*katur tapasya*) and performed austerities and penances to please Lord Shiva. Accepting this as his offering, Lord Shiva appeared before him and asked Ravana to name his boon. Obsessed as he was with power and might, the demon king asked for the boon of invincibility, just as his predecessors, Hiranyaksha, Hiranyakashipu and others of the same ilk had done. Shiva, in His wisdom, gave Ravana an idol, a special Shiva Linga, known as the Atma Linga and told him that he would indeed be invincible, as long as he never allowed the idol to touch the earth's surface. If it did, it would lose its power, whereupon Ravana would become vulnerable to his enemies.

Ravana was very pleased. He carried the Atma Linga with him wherever he went and took for granted the misplaced sense of power that it gave him, committing a great many atrocities against dharma and its true upholders – the sadhus and the rishis. The *devas* were very bitter and carried their complaint to Lord Shiva, but He only gave them an enigmatic smile in reply!

As they were leaving Kailash, their heads hung low in disappointment, they were greeted by Lord Ganesha, who could not bear to see them looking so depressed and disheartened. "Can I be of any help?" he enquired with concern, and the whole story was poured into His sympathetic ears. "Sometimes, your heavenly Father gets carried away, granting boons left and right to these rakshasas," they said to Him bitterly. "He is mightily pleased with their penance and *tapasya* and gives them whatever they ask, before going into His Divine Meditation. We are the ones who pay the price for his generosity. We are tortured, taunted and harassed to no end by the likes of Ravana. What are we to do? Your Father has flatly refused our request. Maybe you will look upon us with a little more compassion."

"I will definitely do whatever I can," Lord Ganesha promised them.

Soon thereafter, Ravana, while on a long journey to the North, stopped at Gokarna for his morning bath. He looked around to see if there was someone to whom he could entrust his precious *Atma Linga* to be held safely while he completed his ablutions. Lord Ganesha appeared before him, in the guise of a cowherd boy. Calling the boy to him, Ravana asked him to hold the idol carefully and instructed him that under no circumstances should it ever be put down. Charming and sweet as ever, Lord Ganesha nodded his head vigorously and took the idol from the demon king.

No sooner had Ravana stepped into the sea for his ritual bath than the little cowherd boy called out urgently, "Come

"Oh no!" cried the merchant, "Not you too! I've lost you forever!"

Grieving, he opened the cage door and lifted the inert form of his beloved pet. He was determined that he would perform its final rites like a father and have a beautiful memorial built for it in his garden.

To his utter amazement, when he took the lifeless parrot out of the cage, it fluttered out of his hand onto the nearest window. From the window sill, it addressed the merchant.

"My kinsman in India was truly wise," it said. "He taught me that the answer to my question was within me! He showed me that the way to attain freedom was through death. I followed his instruction – and now I am free! Please do not try to retain me here. I belong to the wide open spaces, the green trees, the clean air and to the blue skies! I go to find my true home!"

And saying so, the bird fluttered away.

The way to *mukti*, liberation, is through death. Through the death of the body, we gain immortal life. We are released from the golden cage of earthly life, which only restricts and binds us with the chains of maya. Released from the cage, we attain our true state.

POSITIVE VISUALIZATION

Let us begin this session with the chanting of the *pranava* mantra, *Om*.

Now unify your breathing with the repetition of the sacred syllable *Om*. First fill your lungs quickly. Then, as you slowly breathe out, utter the sacred word *Om*. One-third of the utterance should be with parted lips, and the remaining two-thirds with lips closed. This will create a vibration close your eyes to begin the chanting, let the *Mangalamurthi* remain before your inner vision.

Breathe slowly and rhythmically. Chant the mantra softly or as *manana japa* – silently within the heart. Each time you chant, dwell on His Divine features: the broad forehead symbolizes wisdom, the broken tusk which was freely dedicated to the writing of the greatest epic in the world, the snake coiled around His form represents the Divine energy that animates the entire universe, the *modak* held in His hand symbolizes His benevolence, the three-headed *dhruva* grass symbolizes His utter simplicity and His readiness to accept our humblest offerings to Him; and the incongruous little mouse reminds us that we too must control our sense-desires with the help of intellect and inner wisdom.

Chant in silence, as you meditate on the auspicious, benevolent form of Lord Ganesha. His entire form is a symbol of wisdom, power and protection.

Om Gan Ganapataye Namaha!
Om Gan Ganapataye Namaha!
Om Gan Ganapataye Namaha!

As you chant His Name, appeal to Him to take care of you in times of distress. He is the Vighnaharta. He is Vigneshwara. Surrender your cares and difficulties to Him and feel yourself safely wrapped in His Divine protection.

Believe that there is nowhere He cannot reach and there is no obstacle He cannot remove. *Om Gan Ganapataye Namaha!*

As you are engulfed in the warmth of His protection, become aware that Lord Ganesha's blessings of abundance, wisdom and success are upon you.

In the moment of death, we will stand in the radiant presence of God, the Being of Light, who looks on all of us with tender and understanding eyes filled with love. Death is but the return to our Eternal Homeland, the abode of God.

As Lord Krishna says in the *Bhagavad Gita*, the body is only a garment that we have worn. The garment drops down and becomes useless, but the wearer of the garment continues to live. From now on, never say that you will die. It is the physical body that dies. The *jivatman* (the soul that wears the physical body) continues to live in the life that is undying. Once you understand this, you will never be afraid of death. The root cause of our fear is our identification with the physical body. The physical body is only a house in which we dwell for a brief period. When the house crumbles, the tenant of the house still continues to live, but in another house.

Now, while we still inhabit this dwelling here on earth, let us establish a link of love and devotion with God Himself. We must strengthen this link of love and devotion every day. Every day, let us pray to Him, let us cling to His Holy Feet, let us offer all our work to Him and let us in moments of silence converse with Him, with love and intimacy. Let this link bring us closer and closer to God until we feel that wherever we are, we are not far from Him. We are overshadowed by His radiant presence and in His presence there can be no death. For when this body drops down, He will be by us and He will lift us in His loving and everlasting arms, to lead us on – ever onward, forward and Godward.

FREQUENTLY ASKED QUESTIONS (FAQS)

Question: *Is there an ideal state of mind, an attitude that is best suited for mantra* japa?
Answer: It is good to be seated in silence with eyes closed before we begin chanting. This calms the mind and quells needless thoughts. It is also good to remember one's Gurudev, for his grace will surely add to the positive effects of the mantra.

Having said that, I also add that when people take to chanting in a disturbed or anxious state of mind, the initial period of silence helps to calm them down and then the power of the mantra takes over with its beneficial effect.

Question: *Do I need to keep count of the number of chants I utter?*
Answer: This is not always necessary. There are many people who have deep faith in mystical numbers like seven, nine or 108 and so, keep count of the chants. Many others also use the *jap mala* or beaded rosary to keep count. But if you are chanting mantras for peace of mind, it would be enough for you to chant till your agitated mind is calmed and your inner being is filled with peace.

If you do wish to count, let it not be in haste. It must not become mechanical.

Question: *Can I participate in group chanting?*
Answer: Group chanting is a tried and tested process of purification through vocal means. Through the power of the voice, your mind, heart and soul are cleansed, freeing you from negativities, and you find yourself wrapped in the sacred vibrations that emanate from the group chant. The mind and body become resonant with the same positive vibrations. Many practitioners describe this as 'sound healing'.

A Sanskrit verse from the *Brhan-naradiya Purana* states:

Harer nama harer nama harer namaiva kevalam
kalau nasti eva nasti eva nasti eva gatir anyatha

"In this age of *Kali,* there is no alternative, there is no alternative, there is no alternative for spiritual progress other than the chanting of the holy name, the chanting of the holy name, the chanting of the holy name of the Lord."

This great mantra is rooted in what is called *Gaudiya Vaishnavism* and is traced back to the life and teachings of Sri Chaitanya Mahaprabhu. One of his disciples tells us, "Seeing the people of the world afraid of the sins of the age of *Kali* and dejected at heart, Sri Chaitanya Mahaprabhu personally gave them the *Hari-nama* mantra and ordered them to do loud *sankirtana* of this *maha* mantra while dancing and playing musical instruments."

The *Chaitanya Bhagavata* tells us:

"Maha Prabhu (i.e. Sri Chaitanya) ordered everyone in great joy, 'Listen to the *Krishna-nama maha* mantra:

Hare Krishna Hare Krishna Krishna Krishna Hare Hare,
Hare Rama Hare Rama Rama Rama Hare Hare.'

Maha Prabhu: 'I have spoken this *maha* mantra. Perform this *japa* according to the rules. All perfection will be attained through this. Chant this all the time – there is no other rule.'"

Some scholars observe that this is a simple, straightforward mantra or devotional utterance that does not contain words like *Om, namo, Svaha, etc.,* which are subject to several constraints and regulations. All that is uttered here is the Lord's Name in its beauty, glory, divinity and utter simplicity!

We don't need to be Sanskrit scholars; we don't need to be renunciates and ascetics; we don't need to perform complicated rites and rituals; even the most inarticulate among us cannot mispronounce the words in this mantra. All that is needed is for this mantra to be uttered with faith, devotion and *prema bhakti* – loving adoration of the One Who is All Love and deserves all our love!

Stephen Knapp, a Western spiritual practitioner and votary of mantra *japa,* tells us that there are several references to the *maha* mantra in the *Upanishads* and the *Puranas*. He mentions the following in particular:

> *"These sixteen words, Hare Krishna, Hare Krishna, Krishna Krishna, Hare Hare/Hare Rama, Hare Rama, Rama Rama Hare Hare – are especially meant for counteracting the ill effects of the present age of quarrel and anxiety."*
>
> (*Kali-santarana Upanishad*)

> *"All mantras and all processes for self-realization are compressed into the Hare Krishna maha mantra."*
>
> (Narada-pancaratra)

> *"Chant the holy names, chant the holy names, chant the holy names. In this age of Kali [the age of quarrel and confusion] without a doubt there is no other way, there is no other way, there is no other way."*
>
> (*Brihan-naradiya Purana* 38.126)

The *Vishnu-sahasra-nama stotram* states that chanting the Lord's Divine Names has a cleansing, purifying effect on the devotee. Let me give you the *phala sruti* verses at some length, for even reading them is beneficial to one and all:

vaasudevaashrayo martyo vaasudevaparaayanah
sarvapaapa-vishuddhaatmaa yaati brahma sanaatanam

The one who seeks out Lord Vasudeva, looking upon Him as the highest goal to be attained, gets cleansed (purged) of all sins. With a mind thus purified, the chanter attains the eternal *Brahman.*

na vaasudeva bhaktaanaam ashubham vidyate kvachit
janma mrityu jaraavyaadhi bhayam naivopajaayate

Nothing inauspicious ever befalls the devotees of Vasudeva, nor do they have any fear of the cyclic operation of birth, disease, old age and death any longer (with the certain prospect of attaining Him in heaven at the end of the current span of life).

imam stava-madhiiyaanah shraddhaa bhakti samanvita
yujyetaatma-sukha-kshaanti shri-dhriti-smriti-kirtanirtibhih

The chanter of this hymn, who demonstrates zeal and devotion, is blest with the happy realization of the essential nature of the Self (svasvarupa), besides the qualities of serenity, mental stability, unfailing memory and great fame and wealth (put to beneficial use).

> *of full consciousness, because that gives one a start in searching after his supreme interest.'"*
>
> (*Srimad Bhagavatam* 2.1.11-13)

Rama-tapaniyopanisad (1.6) explains the meaning of the *maha* mantra as follows:

> The Lord is known as Hari because He takes away the sins and three types of suffering accumulated over millions of births, of those who remember Him. The root krs indicates the supreme attractiveness of the Lord, the suffix na indicates the supreme joy. Therefore, the name Krsna indicates the Supreme Brahman who is the acme of these two characteristics.
>
> The yogis take pleasure in the Supreme Self, which is existence, knowledge and bliss absolute. Therefore, that truth, known as the *Param Brahman* is also called *Rama.*

Some say that the current popularity of this ancient mantra, which has been recited in India for a long time, is due to the fact that Swami Bhaktivedanta Prabhupâda bequeathed it to the disciples of the Hare Krishna Movement, thereby making its power and energy known to a worldwide audience. Swamiji also encouraged the constant repetition and *japa* of this sacred mantra, which he felt would raise us to the level of Krishna Consciousness. As a result of this, the mantra lent its name to the worldwide Hare Krishna Movement, one of the modern offshoots of the Hindu faith.

What can I tell you about the meaning and power of this Divine mantra? I doubt that there is even one among my readers who has not recited it or any who have not been happy to hear it recited by the devout! In any case, the Name upheld as the means of salvation by Maharishi Narada, the *Sanakadi* rishis, Prahlada and Dhruva. It is the Name of Lord Narayana!

Those of us who are trapped in the maya of worldly desires ask Him for many things: more money, a job, marriage, landed property, promotion or success in examinations or business ventures, but the Lord is not unaware of human needs. He knows that there are some of us who are *artha bhaktas* (devotees who desire worldly rewards). He grants them to us, if they are good for us. After all, He is our Divine Father! To whom can we turn, if not to our Father, to fulfill all our needs, worldly or otherwise?

We can ask Him for all we need, but let us also remember that it is He and He alone who can bestow on us a rare and precious gift that no one else can give us – the great gift of Liberation!

Om Namo Bhagavate Vasudevaya is held up to us as a *mukti* mantra, a mantra for liberation. Our sages and saints extol its power as 'a potent spiritual formula' for attaining freedom. Dear friends, may I tell you that if we are so fortunate and so blessed to have this Name on our lips today, it is because we have gone through countless births, crossed innumerable whirlpools of life and death, perhaps even put in several lives of *tapasya* and prayer, that we might have the privilege of uttering the Name Divine and clinging to the Name as our passport to freedom! It is a hard-earned gift! Constant repetition of this mantra, aloud or within the heart, will eventually free us from the cycles of rebirth, even if it's over a multitude of incarnations! It is a mantra of liberation, because it can free us from the bonds of lower desires and inculcate in us a true longing for the Divine. It is a mantra that will help us make the right choice, not the choice of the *dwandas* or the binary opposites of worldly life, but the ultimate choice of moksha, oneness with the Lord!

Vasudeva is a deeply symbolic Name. Scholars quote our ancient scriptures to explain the name as *Vasanthi Asmin Sarvani Bhutani Ithi* – *Vasu* is the one in whom all beings reside; and *Vasanthi ayam dehe ithi* – He who resides in all jivas or beings. *Deva* as in *Divu kreda ithi* refers to the One for whom the acts of creation, sustenance and destruction are mere play. In short, the term refers to One who permeates all that is.

Sanskrit, as we have seen, is a beautiful and profound language, and several other symbolic meanings are attributed to this Name Divine. *Vasudha* refers to the Universe or to the entire Creation, the vast cosmos in which our planet is but a speck of a speck of a speck. *Eva* is translated to mean 'certainly' or 'verily'. Therefore, the *Vedas* give us the beautiful saying: *vasudaiva kutumbakam,* which means that the entire world is truly just one family. It also relates to the Lord of the Universe, Vasudeva, who is none other than Lord Krishna.

But speaking personally, what makes this Name very dear to me is that the Lord of the Universe who dwells in all things, and to whom the entire act of creation is but child's play, is He who also dwells in the lotus of my own heart.

Lord Krishna tells us in the *Gita*:

> *Vasudevah sarvam iti sa mahatma sudurlabhah. (VII -19)*

In other words, "Rare and difficult to find, is the great soul who knows that Vasudeva is All!"

Need I say more?

The Transformative Power of the *Maha* Mantra

Sant Haridasa Thakur was born into a brahmana family. His parents passed away when he was a small child; a devout Muslim family then took him in and raised him. But very early in life, Haridas Thakur took *diksha* according to his own statement written in *Chaitanya Charitamrita*:

sankhya-nama-sankirtana– ei maha-yajna manye
tahate diksita ami ha-i prati-dine

> I have on initiation, vowed to perform everyday a great sacrifice of a numerical count of chanting the Holy Name.

It is described in the same biography that he was named '*Nama Brahma Haridas*' because of his fixation for chanting the *maha* mantra 300,000 times! Within the *Gaudiya Vaisnava* tradition, the Hare Krishna *maha* mantra is known as '*Tarak-Brahma-Nama*' or 'the Mantra that delivers All'. One would think the name *Nama Brahma Haridas* is in relationship with the chanting of this mantra.

In the *Chaitanya Bhagavat* we are told:

> People would gather around him (Haridas Thakur) just to see the unrestricted tears of love of Godhead that flowed profusely from his eyes drenching his entire body. Even the strictest atheists marveled at his behaviour. Goose pimples swelled across his body like thousands of blooming flowers and even Lord Brahma and Lord Shiva were amazed by his devotion!

Once, Sant Haridas was staying in a village and his nightly chanting of the *maha* mantra angered a chieftain, who wanted to bring the saint into disrepute by any means, fair or foul. He called the most beautiful and sought after prostitute in the region and told her to seduce the saint: "Bring him under your spell. Enslave him by your charms and I will give you one half of all my landed property," he told her.

The prostitute smiled derisively. "There is no man who will not fall victim to my charms," she drawled. "Just show me where he lives, and in less than three days, I will have him eating out of my hands!"

That night, she called at the humble cottage of Haridas Thakur. She walked into the hut uninvited, and said to the saint, "I have come to spend an unforgettable night with you."

"You are most welcome," said the saint. "But it is my sacred vow to chant the *maha* mantra 300,000 times every night. Please wait outside while I complete my chanting."

All night the fallen woman sat at the saint's doorstep. The chanting of the *maha* mantra fell on her ears and she was filled with a sense of awe and wonder...

The next day dawned and she hastened home, promising

day come to occupy a prime place in his father's heart. But the Lord's *darshan* wrought a tremendous transformation upon his soul. The constant repetition of the mantra had kindled his highest aspirations. With folded hands and head bowed, Dhruva said to the Lord, "I want neither the reins of power, nor the pleasures of this earth. I want Thee and Thee alone!"

The Lord so blessed Dhruva, that he was transformed into the most steadfast star on the horizon – the Pole Star. The boy, who had been pushed away from his father's knee, became the Beloved of the Lord. As the Pole Star, the *Dhruva-Nakshatra,* he shines on steadily, not moving from his place, come summer or winter!

Dhruva is indeed, the shining example of *bhakti* yoga!

POSITIVE VISUALIZATION

Sit in a silent corner at a peaceful time. Gently close your eyes and prepare to invoke the Divine Presence of Lord Vishnu. It may be any form of Lord Narayana, it may be Lord Rama or Lord Krishna.

He is not a shadowy being. He is Here and Now!

It is His Divine intention (*bhagavat sankalpa*) to take care of you and protect you, just as a father would.

As you repeat the Name Divine, recall your true and eternal relationship with Him.

Begin by taking a deep breath and follow the breath with the mantra resonating within you.

Om Namo Bhagavate Vasudevaya!

Visualize that you are cradled in a world that is on fire. Just like *Bhakta* Prahlad, you are surrounded by the karmic

He is Jaya Rama – the Victorious One. He carries His invincible bow for our protection, not His! He is Sita Rama, the beloved husband of Sita. He is the Bestower of grace, blessings and absolute protection to those who seek it from Him. He is the Soul of integrity and virtue, who never ever abandons those who seek His refuge.

Dwell on His Divine qualities:

Hare Rama Hare Rama Rama Rama Hare Hare Hare Krishna Hare Krishna Krishna Krishna Hare Hare

Krishna! Even as you utter His name, there is music in the air! The Divine melody of the flute wafts in with the cool breeze, as you see yourself on the banks of the Yamuna. When you see Him, the irrepressible Child playing out His Divine *leela* in Gokul, you watch mesmerized as the Gopis swoon in their adoration of the charming Lad. You see Him playing the flute, the inscrutable smile on his lips, the enchanting Lord who captures the hearts of everyone who looks on Him. Allow your heart to be stolen, as easily as the butter he stole away. Feel your soul melting as it dissolves in devotion to the Thief of all hearts and souls!

Feel the form of Lord Rama merging into the form of Lord Krishna. The King of Ayodhya and the Divine Cowherd of Gokul are one and the same! The Conqueror of Lanka and the *Maakan Chhor* of Brindaban are one and the same! He who lived the principle of dharma, and he who taught the essence of dharma are one and the same!

Hare Rama! Hare Rama! Destroy all that is evil and negative in our lives!

Hare Krishna! Hare Krishna! I surrender myself unto you!

Question: *Many declare proudly that they have chanted a mantra 1000 times today. Does such an attitude towards chanting help in any way?*
Answer: Any kind of chanting, any number of times, never goes in vain. However, boasting about it is surely not good! Metaphorically speaking, if you wish to turn the beads of the rosary, you need to be as humble as ash and dust, as forbearing as a tree and honour others without seeking any honours for yourself.

A Mantra for Lord Shiva

Om Namah Shivaya!

I bow to Lord Shiva!
Adoration to Lord Shiva!

Known among the devout as the *panchakshara* or five-syllable mantra, this is also venerated as the mantra for redemption. The five syllables *na, ma, shi, va* and *ya,* are said to represent the five elements – earth, water, fire, air and space. The chanting of the *panchakshara* mantra with intense devotion can bring before us the vision of Kailashnath.

And what a magnificent form it is! The *Puranas* tell us that when Lord Shiva appeared in the traditional *baaraat* or marriage procession to wed Parvati, the daughter of King Himawaan, her mother wept in anger and disappointment on seeing the ascetic figure smeared in ashes, who had captured the heart of her beautiful daughter. It was Lord Vishnu, who explained Lord Shiva's power and magnificence to the ignorant queen, and assured her that her son-in-law was a Supreme Being whose nature transcended appearances.

Shaivite scholars tell us that Lord Shiva's outward appearance is a reminder of the fundamental truth of Hindu addressing one specific Hindu deity, it offers worship to the God of Light or Wisdom.

Attributed originally to Sage Vishwamitra, the *Gayatri* mantra is found in the *Rig Veda,* but it is also cited in scriptures like the *Harivamsa* and the *Bhagavad Gita*. "Among all mantras, I am the *Gayatri*," Lord Krishna declares in the *Gita,* emphasizing its prominence and its value as a prayer. One unique attribute of this mantra, is that it is found in all four of the *Vedas,* in the same form and with the same content. Therefore, the *Gayatri* is referred to as *Vedamata* or the Mother of the *Vedas.*

As with so many of our Vedic hymns, translations are unable to do adequate justice in capturing the profoundity and intensity of this ancient invocation. However, I would like to share the free renderings made by some of the most eminent scholars and philosophers:

Swami Vivekananda paraphrases the mantra as:

> We meditate on the glory of that Being who has produced this universe; may He enlighten our minds.

Dr. Sarvepalli Radhakrishnan offers two interpretations:

> We meditate on the effulgent glory of the Divine Light; may He inspire our understanding. Or, "We meditate on the adorable glory of the radiant sun; may He inspire our intelligence."

The members of the Arya Samaj follow this interpretation:

> O God! Giver of life, Remover of all pain and sorrows, Bestower of happiness, the Creator of the Universe, Thou art most luminous, adorable and the destroyer of sins. We meditate upon thee. May

> thou inspire, enlighten and guide our intellect in the right direction.

The Brahmo Samaj interpretation runs thus:

> We meditate on the adorable power and glory of Him who has created the earth, the nether world and the heavens (i.e. the whole universe), and who directs our understanding.

All these interpretations affirm that the *Gayatri* mantra is essentially a prayer for clear thinking and ensuring the correct use of our God-given intelligence. Our scriptures have taught us that ignorance or *avidya, ajnana* is the darkness of the mind and the cause of all of man's suffering. This is true of philosophy, spirituality and day-to-day living. The *Gayatri* mantra is an invocation to the Supreme Being to lead us out of the darkness of ignorance and into the realm of light.

Our ancient scriptures tell us, *Asavadityo Brahma* – the Sun is the visible form of the Supreme Being, Lord Brahman; that is why the *Gayatri* mantra is addressed to the source of light. After all, Divinity is best symbolized by light!

When I speak of clear thinking and applied intelligence, I mean the awakening of the wisdom that is intuitive and must come from within us, not prompted or promoted by external sources. It is this intuition that is referred to in our scriptures as *buddhi, manas,* etc. This mantra directly invokes the God of Light to awaken our intelligence from within.

Following the *pranava* mantra *Om,* we come across a reference to three distinct terms known as the *Mahavyahriti* or great utterance: *bhūr bhuvah svah.* These are variously interpreted to mean 1) the three Hindu worlds of the

Permit me to share a beautiful and profoundly simple English rendering of this *stotra* sent to me by a friend:

> I am not the mind, intellect, thought, ego or some form of the Supreme Being; I neither have ears, nor a tongue and I neither have nostrils, nor eyes; I am not the sky, earth, light or the wind; I am the fortunate, joyful, Supreme Being who is the very emblem of truth, knowledge and eternal bliss. I am consciousness and bliss. I am Shiva, I am Shiva.

I don't have to tell you that the sloka that I just shared with you is from Sri Adi Shankara's immortal hymn, *Atmashatakam* – the song of the Self. As we can see, the speaker in this hymn can be thought to be Lord Shiva, as the constant refrain, *Shivoham, Shivoham* (I am Shiva, I am Shiva) indicates. It can equally be the song of the soul, the immortal atman within each one of us, which realizes its oneness with the Supreme Self and thus, asserts the essential principle of advaita philosophy – I am that: *Aham Brahmasmi*. The atman is pure consciousness, pure bliss and by implication, the atman and *Brahman* are One.

Adi Shankara said that the very utterance of the Name Shiva purifies the one who utters it. His immortal *Atmashtakam* is a hymn which glorifies this true Self, the Divine Principle that dwells within us and links us directly with Lord Shiva.

We live in an age of haste. People have neither the time nor patience to listen, wait, reflect or sit still. Modern man is basically a restless creature. His mind knows no peace and his thoughts race with the speed of lightning.

many parts of the country, *Upanayanam* is also referred to as *Gayatri diksha*. After this ceremony, the initiate is supposed to recite the *Gayatri* mantra at sunrise and sunset everyday, for the welfare of the world.

In certain circles, it was held that the *Gayatri* mantra was not to be recited aloud, but only in its *manasika* or silent, mental form. Some people also believed that the mantra should not be recited by the uninitiated and definitely not by women. But the fact of the matter is the power and intensity of the people's devotion and faith have over-ridden such restrictions today. The many Hindu reform movements and the modern *kirtan* and chanting movements have rejected caste and gender restrictions. Therefore, chanting, singing, reciting and listening to the chanting of this mantra is the mainstay of several group *kirtans* and *satsangs* today.

Swami Vivekananda, who spearheaded the Hindu Renaissance among the youth, began initiating non-Brahmins with the Sacred Thread Ceremony and the *Gayatri* mantra in 1898. He cited the authority of the *Gita* that the status of a Brahmin is earned based on one's attitude, thoughts and practices, and not reserved by birth or heredity for a select few. For its part, the Arya Samaj too encouraged the notion that the recitation of the mantra was not limited to men, and that women could rightfully be taught the *Vedas* and the *Gayatri* mantra. Dr. S. Radhakrishnan, the great scholar, statesman and philosopher concurred that the *Gayatri* mantra should be taught to men and women of all castes.

All the great Gurus and spiritual teachers of this modern age encourage listening to this sacred mantra or chanting it. It is believed that the very sound of its *shabda* can protect us

Shiva is My True Self

The Sufi masters tell us that there are three journeys on the road to self-realization. During the first journey, man wanders endlessly and moves away from reality. The restless mind pushes man to the pleasures of the world and man gets caught in worldly affairs, forgetting the purpose of his journey.

A story in the *Shiva Purana* describes a similar situation. At the height of her wedded bliss in Mount Kailash, Goddess Parvati said to Lord Shiva one day, "O Lord, I desire this one thing above all else – to be by your side always! I wish to serve you with devotion. I desire nothing else. I will keep vigil when you are in the state of *samadhi*. When you choose to rest, I will press your feet. The sole purpose of my existence is to serve you. I only beg this of you, please allow me to be forever by your side."

Lord Shiva granted his consort the boon she desired. And so, Goddess Parvati lived with Lord Shiva on Mount Kailash for many centuries. One day, however, She developed the desire to step beyond Her limited routine and leave her snowy residence. She was filled with the urge to go out, see the world and experience its pleasures and sensual delights.

She promptly expressed this urge to Her Lord. "My

Lord," She said to Him, "kindly permit me to take a short trip beyond this domain." In response, Lord Shiva reminded Her of the promise She had made to serve Him and always be by His side. But She countered by saying, "I do remember my promise. It is just that I want to have some experience of other things, too. I will go out and experience the world for a short while, while you sit in meditation here. As you have been preaching the wisdom of detachment, can you not allow me to be away from you for a short while? Our devotees will be upset if they find out that you are so attached to me, that you refuse to let go of me, even for a little while."

Goddess Parvati was firm and adamant. Lord Shiva, therefore, said to Her, "If you wish to go, you may definitely do so." Goddess Parvati was excited and thrilled. "I shall be away only for a short while," She said to Her Lord. "You may go into your *samadhi* and I shall return by the time you are out of your meditation." She then waited patiently until Lord Shiva began his meditation.

No sooner did He close His eyes, than She set out on Her journey. From one village to another, from one town to another, She travelled far. Everywhere She went, crowds of devotees thronged around Her. She was welcomed with flowers, garlands and other offerings of love and devotion. Wherever She went, Her devotees followed Her eagerly. She was overwhelmed by their devotion and reverence. She was so enchanted by the honours and the gifts bestowed upon Her that She did not miss the presence of Her beloved Lord Shiva.

As She wandered further on, She reached South India. It was then that She felt the absence of Lord Shiva. She realized that She had been away from Her Lord's abode for too long.

creature for he was a king, and his needs were many, and (he felt) needed to be fulfilled promptly.

You are familiar with the undignified tussle which followed. Kaushika used all his military might and power to wrest the calf away from the sage's ashram, but Vashishta's power was the power of *tapasya,* so it decimated Kaushika's army. The sons and generals of Kaushika who laid violent hands on Nandini were turned into ashes by the Divine calf, who was now given permission to use her powers to protect herself from harm. Unable to take this bitter defeat, King Kaushika renounced his kingdom and his crown to undertake a life of austerity – so that he would, one day, acquire more power than Vashishta.

Driven by ego, arrogance and the bitterness of a defeated man, Kaushika did not realize the negativity of his approach. He was only filled with the burning desire to outdo, outwit and outsmart Sage Vashishta in every way possible. This being his attitude, his *khator tapasya* always ended in disaster. Once, he lost his temper; another time, he tried to use his yogic powers to assist a king in ascending to heaven with his physical body; the third time, the *devas* sent an *apsara* to seduce him and he lost self-control. Not once, but several times did he stumble and fall on the path of *tapasya*. But to his credit, he did not give up, and gradually, his pride and ego gave way to genuine quest and devotion. After being subjected to several tests, Kaushika proved his worth and Lord Brahma appeared before him to bless him and designate him as a Maharishi. Vashishta, the sage whom he had previously looked upon as a rival, pronounced that Kaushika was indeed a Brahmarishi. The *Gayatri* mantra was then revealed to Kaushika, who generously shared it with one and all for the benefit of the world; that is how he came to be known as Vishwamitra – a friend to the world!

Let me close with a very dramatic rendering of this ending, as narrated in some versions: Having received Brahma's grace, we are told, Kaushika goes straight to Sage Vashishta's ashram. He picks up a huge boulder and lifts it above his head with the superhuman strength now available to him. In anger and hatred he waits, determined to crush Sage Vashishta to death by dropping the boulder on him the moment he steps out of his ashram.

Moments pass, when he hears a conversation between Sage Vashishta and his wife, Arundhati. It is about him! Arundhati asks her husband, "Do you think that Kaushika deserves to be known as a Brahmarishi?"

"Think? I don't have to think in order to answer that question. I know Kaushika is deserving of that honour in every way. He has had to struggle to attain this status, and that makes his efforts all the more commendable. I feel that he is about to succeed! Although, my dear wife, I feel instinctively that there is something, one last obstacle which stands in his way even now! However, I know that he is sure to overcome this too, just as he overcame his other negative karmas!"

Kaushika is profoundly moved. A great transformation comes over him and the huge boulder slips harmlessly from his hands. The door of the *kutiya* opens and Sage Vashishta steps out. Kaushika falls at his feet and as his head touches the holy feet of the sage, the sacred *Gayatri* mantra is revealed to him!

Therefore, it is believed that uttering this mantra with faith can destroy all our sins and wipe out all our negative karmas of accumulated births!

Answer: A Guru can initiate a disciple by a touch or a gaze, or through meditation.

Question: *Some gurus give a common mantra to a group of disciples. Can that one mantra help them all?*
Answer: Giving the mantra in the way it is given nowadays, I think, is of very little help. The mantra is to be given only after a disciple has passed many tests and trials. There are gurus who will not give you a mantra for years together until they feel sure that you are a person who is truly worthy of the mantra. Such a person is called *paatra.*

Question: *At what age can a person benefit from the chanting of a mantra? How young can one be?*
Answer: It depends on the individual. Age is no barrier for the chanting of a mantra.

surrounding you; feel the radiance that fills your mind; feel the all-giving, all-loving, all-healing energy of the Divine Being of which you are also a part!

Continue chanting till you are at peace and the mind has reached stillness.

Thank the Divine Mother Gayatri!

FREQUENTLY ASKED QUESTIONS (FAQS)

Question: *Does it help the family if the partners/children chant the mantras together?*
Answer: If all the family members, from the youngest to the eldest, meet together at a fixed time and chant the mantra, it does help. It creates a new climate in the home and solves many problems.

Question: *If a pregnant mother chants mantras, can it positively influence an unborn child?*
Answer: It all depends on the child and the karma it brings with itself. If the child is receptive, it will help him even in the embryo stage.

Question: *Will it help the dying husband if the wife chants mantras at his bedside?*
Answer: Yes. It is always advisable to chant a mantra near a dying person. It will help him and the rest of the family.

Question: *Is there any relationship between the sound of the mantra and the chakras located throughout the body?*
Answer: Yes. But only in the case of a few mantras, not all.

an easy and effortless way to recite the thousand Names of Lord Vishnu:

> *Keno payena laguna Vishnor nama sahasrakam patyate*
> *panditair nityam shrotumicchamyaham prabho*

To translate it freely:

> I desire to hear from my Lord the means by which scholars can recite in an abridged manner the thousand names of Lord Vishnu every day.

Graciously acknowledging her as a disciple, Lord Shiva teaches her the following mantra:

> *Sri Rama Rama Raameti*
> *Rame Raame Manorame*
> *Sahasranama Tattulyam*
> *Raama Nama Varaanane*

> Uttering the Divine *Rama Naam* just thrice is equivalent to reciting the entire *Sahasranama.*

There are 1,008 Names of the Lord, each as sweet as nectar, as precious as diamonds or rubies and as powerful as a pass that will grant us instant access to heaven! *Keshava, Madhava, tujya naam matre godva* sings the Marathi poet, and we would all heartily agree with his view – there is nectar in each of His thousand Names. And yet, what is so significant about these two syllables *Ra* and *Ma*?

All other mantras, except the *pranava* mantra, are based on one or other of the names Divine; and yet the *Rama Naam* mantra alone is held up to us as the *taraka* mantra – that which helps us cross the Ocean of Samsara.

Payo ji maine, Rama ratan dhan payo, sings that ultimate

devotee of Lord Krishna, our own immortal saint Mira. It translates to mean: I acquired the invaluable gem which is the treasure of *Rama Naam*!

We talk about three different planes of *bhakti*, offered to three different concepts of the Supreme, namely: the *nirguna Brahman* (Formless), *saguna Brahman* (One with a Form) and meditation on the Abstract Principle of the Divine. The sacred *Rama Naam* mantra is equally as precious as all the three forms of *bhakti*!

Erudite practitioners of Kundalini yoga tell us that the syllable *Ra* is the link to our *mooladhara* chakra (the root chakra), while the syllable *ma* is directly connected to the *sahasrara* chakra (the destination or crown chakra), which integrates all other chakras and represents the highest level of perception that each of us is capable of. Therefore, they tell us that the repetition of the *Rama Naam* in all faith and concentration arouses the kundalini shakti and carries it directly to its destination. By the proper chanting of this mantra, one can actually become a yogi.

Here is an algebraic calculation used by a witty speaker to emphasize the *mahima* of the *Rama Naam*: the chief mantra for pious Vaishnavaites is the *Ashtakshara* (*Om Namo Narayana*); for the devout Shaivites it is the *Panchakshara* (*Om Nama Shivay*). Here is his ingenuity in explication: Without the letter *ra,* he argues, *Narayana* would read as *Nayana*. This means one without a way to go (*gati*). Similarly, without the letter *ma, Namashivay* would read as *Nashivaya,* which as many of us may or may not know actually means 'inauspicious'. So, he concludes triumphantly, these two syllables *ra* and *ma* are actually the *jiva akshara* (life-giving letters)! *Ra* and *Ma,* the *jiva aksharas* of the two sacred him, Markandeya continued to practice his austerities and study of the scriptures.

On the eve of his 16th birthday, his distraught mother could contain herself no longer. Weeping uncontrollably, she revealed the truth about his birth as a boon from Lord Shiva and the destiny that they themselves had chosen for their beloved son. "It is your 16th birthday tomorrow, and you will be taken away from us!" she sobbed.

Markandeya consoled his parents. "Dear Father and Mother, you chose right for me! Of what use is a long but undistinguished life devoid of *bhakti* and enlightenment? I thank you and I thank the Lord who has blessed me with piety and devotion. Do not weep, dear mother, for Lord Shiva is the Lord of Death! He will protect me from all harm and He will certainly not let you come to grief!"

On his 16th birthday, Markandeya began to perform a Shiva Pooja from dawn. Sitting with his eyes closed before a Shiva *Lingam*, he chanted the *maha mrityunjaya* mantra and began to focus all his concentration on Rudra, his *ishta devata*. As twilight approached, Yama, the Lord of Death arrived to take away his life, as had been destined by Lord Shiva. "Come on, lad, your time upon this earth is over," he said to the young yogi, deep in meditation. But Markandeya was lost in devotion, so he paid no attention to Yama's presence or his call. Incensed by this, Yama hurled a noose at him and it accidentally entwined Markandeya with the Shiva Lingam that he was worshipping! Out of the bound Lingam a furious Lord Shiva emerged, enraged at the insult to his form and the disrespect offered to his devotee. He trounced Yama almost to the point of death, stopping short of destroying him only because the *devas* intervened and begged him to have mercy on the god, who was only doing his duty. Shiva relented and Yama was spared on the condition that he would never ever approach Markandeya. The young sage was thus bestowed with the gift of immortality. It is believed that he still lives, frequenting shrines and mingling with the devout in disguise.

Symbolically, the legend signifies that Markandeya was a *jivan-mukta,* a blessed soul who had attained liberation through God's grace. He had attained oneness with the Supreme Being and was freed from the cycle of birth and death.

The episode of Lord Shiva's encounter with Yama is commemorated as *Kala samharam* or Destruction of Death in the *Shiva Purana* and the *Skanda Purana.*

The *maha mrityunjaya* mantra is hailed by the sages as the very heart of the *Vedas.* Along with the *Gayatri* mantra, it holds a position of pre-eminence among the many mantras chanted by the devout.

When people set out on long journeys or undertake difficult expeditions, they chant this mantra to guard themselves from accidents and dangers. When loved ones fall ill, have to be hospitalized or undergo surgery, their family members chant this mantra to help them heal and get better sooner.

This mantra is also chanted to pray for departed souls, so that their spirits may reach their heavenly abode and rest at the Lotus Feet of the Lord. By the same token, it is also a force that guides lost souls who have been taken away by sudden unnatural deaths, such as fatal accidents. It is no exaggeration to say that this is indeed a mantra of conquest, a conquest over the Self and over death.

Rama Naam ki Mahima

In one of the *Puranas,* we come across an instance where the *devas* and deities had an issue of the ego, which led to a serious struggle. The issue lay in deciding who was the most powerful deity among them. Every deity blew his own trumpet, highlighting his shakti. The matter could not be settled because each one was trying to top the other! It was finally decided that all the deities would request Lord Brahma, the All-knowing One, to act as their Judge and Referee. "Lord, it is you who must use your Divine Judgement to pronounce who is the most superior one among us," They told him.

Lord Brahma replied, "To know who is the most superior among you, all of you will have to go through a test. I do not want to favour anyone or recommend anyone. Let your own actions prove your superiority." He then gave them the details of the event in which all of them would have to compete: They were to take a full round or circumambulate the Universe. Whosoever finished first would be declared the winner and the most superior among the deities.

All the deities rushed to complete the task. As you know, each deity has his own vehicle and according to the *Puranas,* Lord Ganesha mounted his mouse... but unfortunately, he was unable to start the journey. Wise as He was, He sought experience. Many great mahatmas have assured us that it can actually be a very pleasant experience. Now, if death is a pleasant experience, then it stands to reason that we must conquer the fear of death and free ourselves from its obsessive hold on our psyche – that is what this mantra can help us accomplish!

When we live in this spirit of *vairagya* or detachment, the inescapable phases of this mortal life, such as growth, old age, death and decay cease to trouble us. We become aware of what I call the First Commandment of the *Gita*:

You are not this perishable body that you wear, you are the immortal atman!

Identification with the body leads to the illusion that the power, pleasures and possessions of this world can make us happy. But this is not true; instead, these material possessions only keep us in bondage – the bondage of ignorance, *avidya*. Once you are freed from this illusion, you will realize the truth of the Self and move towards the realization of God. This is the process by which we may all move from illusion to reality, from darkness to light and from death to eternity.

Is this not a beautiful attitude to cultivate? It becomes possible with the regular chanting of this mantra:

Let us not be afraid of death, for there is light at the end of the tunnel. We should not be scared during the last few moments of our life, for the messengers of God come to take us away through the tunnel of death into the sphere of light. The face of a person who dies often shines; it is calm and peaceful. The soul is liberated from the heavy burden of the worn-out garment, which was formally known as the body.

We should not be afraid of death; on the contrary, we should reflect on this wonderful phenomenon that takes leprosy and I was told that if I catch a glimpse of Sant Kabir, I would be cured of my disease."

Loi replied, "Sant Kabir has gone out, but it is not difficult to cure you of your illness. If you would chant with me, just three times, the Divine Name of *Rama,* you would be free from the disease." Loi began to recite the Name of *Rama* and the leper repeated it after her. As he did so, his disease receded and he was completely cured in no time. Pleased with the miracle, the beggar left in a hurry without even waiting to thank Sant Kabir.

On Sant Kabir's return, Loi narrated the incident to him. Sant Kabir said, "Where was the need to chant the Name of *Rama* three times? Once would have been sufficient!"

To this Loi replied, "It is true. With the very first utterance of the Name *Rama,* the man was cured. But I visualized this man getting the same disease in his next two births and so I thought to myself, why not relieve him from the suffering of his next two births right now?"

Such is the power of the word *Rama.*

Utter the Name *Rama* with devotion and you will be cleansed of all sin and evil.

POSITIVE VISUALIZATION

As you sit in silence and begin reciting the powerful *Rama Naam,* let Him enter your mind, heart and soul. Call to Him with love and great longing.

Rama... Rama... Rama... Let those magical musical vibrations fill your being with light!

Hold the magnificent vision of Raja Rama before your

eyes. Lord Rama is an Avatar of Perfection. He is the *Maryada Purushottam,* the epitome of righteousness!

As you continue reciting the *Rama Naam,* let the well-known, well-beloved *Ramayana* legend unfold before your mind's eye. He walked this earth, He lived as one among ordinary mortals like us, He suffered and triumphed. He actually wept and despaired, loved and laughed and went through all the shocks and sufferings that ordinary mortals are subjected to. In His abundant love for us, He came to show us how we, too, can embody the Divine on Earth; how we may live our lives in accordance with dharma and the Divine principles.

As we recount His life, let us entreat Him to grace us with each of His Divine qualities.

As we chant *"Rama, Rama, Rama"* in our depths, let us dwell upon His courage; let us think of His devotion to duty and His absolute, unquestioning obedience to the Guru; let us dwell on His filial love and piety; let us appreciate His commitment to truth and justice; and finally, let us bow down to His selflessness and compassion for the tiniest and humblest of creatures. Let us marvel at His self-sacrifice!

Let us pray that He may so bless us that some of His Divine qualities may touch our being.

Rama, Rama, Rama!

FREQUENTLY ASKED QUESTIONS (FAQS)

Question: *How did the mantra originate?*
Answer: Each mantra originated in a different way. Some of them were heard in periods of deep meditation, while others were uttered by sages in periods of ecstasy and inspiration.

The merchant laughed loudly, as he fed delicious berries to the parrot. “I can give you the answer to your question, precious pet,” he said, not in anger, but in love. “I will never ever let you go – so much for your freedom! Have I not given you a golden cage? Do I not feed you with the choicest tidbits that you love? Do I not love you even as I love my own children? Why can’t you enjoy the comfort and security of my palatial home and be happy with your life here? Why do you want freedom? What will you do with freedom?”

“Whatever it may be, I would like you to find the answer to my question,” insisted the parrot. “Let us say, it is of academic interest to me.”

“Very well, I promise,” the merchant assured him. “I will definitely talk to your brothers and sisters in India and bring you back the answer you seek; mind you, for academic interest only! For I will never let you go.”

The merchant kept his word. Having finished his business in India and having bought gifts for his family, he visited the holy city of Varanasi about which he had heard a lot. Here, on the banks of the holy river Ganga, he found a flock of parrots seated on a parapet wall. He decided to address his pet’s question to these birds.

“Tell me, parrots, for one of your kin who lives with me wants to know this from you: *how can he attain his freedom?*”

At the mention of the word freedom, the parrots flew away, as if to prove their love for that very idea. Only one parrot, the leader of the flock, remained before the merchant. He looked deep into the eyes of the merchant, almost mesmerizing him.

“How may he attain his freedom?” the merchant repeated, his eyes locked with the eyes of the bird.

Without uttering a word, the parrot dropped down lifeless before the stunned gaze of the merchant. He lay on the ground inert and dead, a heap of green feathers.

The merchant was shocked and grieved. "I should not have asked that question," he thought to himself. "It was a terrible blunder on my part."

When he returned home, he was received by his family with great joy. When everyone had received their gifts, he sent them all away and came to talk to his pet, all alone.

"Well?" said the bird. "Did you get the answer to my question?"

"I really should not have done it," said the merchant with a heavy heart. "I found a lovely group of your kin on the banks of the holy river Ganga. I put your question before them, and they all flew away except one – the leader of the flock."

"What did he say?" asked the bird eagerly.

"That's just it," said the merchant. "He did not say a word! He just dropped down, dead! Oh, it was unbearable – I wish I had not asked him!"

"Never mind what you felt," said the parrot. "Tell me exactly what happened."

Patiently, the merchant narrated the incident exactly as it had happened: how the parrot had stared silently at him, how he had repeated the question and how the bird had fallen before his very eyes, lifeless!

"Why are you so obsessed with the idea of freedom?" he asked his pet. "What does it mean to you?"

The parrot stared at him wordlessly. Then, it fell from its perch in the golden cage and lay in a lifeless heap on the floor of the cage.

Like so many of our great mantras, this is not a request for worldly gains. The *jignasu* or seeker realizes the limitations of the human life which binds his atman and asks the Supreme Being for transcendence – to rise above the mortal coils through the purificatory power of the chant. Therein lies the significance of its name: the *pavamana abhyaroha* mantra cleanses and purifies us from within and helps us ascend to the highest level of consciousness.

The word *sat* used here is not just truth as we use it in legal or ethical terms, such as the truth of the law or the rule-book. It is the great concept of Ultimate Reality – that which was, that which is and that which will ever be! It is the Truth of the Divine Being, that which alone is. When we become conscious of this great Truth, all else falls into place and the darkness of *avidya* vanishes, as does the fear of the illusion called death.

How may we vanquish the falsehood, the darkness and destruction that seem to overwhelm us wherever we turn? How may we move from darkness to light? Quite simply by kindling the light! If each of us were to light a little lamp, a tiny flame, the darkness would be instantly dispelled, would it not? But we also need to kindle another light – the lamp that is within us, the light that can illuminate our heart and soul; the light that will lead us on to self- knowledge and ultimate liberation, the light of the truth about the atman, the great truth of human existence!

Knowledge is the greatest light of all. But when I say knowledge, it does not mean textbook knowledge. In fact, the world is greatly advanced in the pursuit of external knowledge, that is, the knowledge of science and technology. What we need to focus on is another kind of knowledge –

within you. Do this three times. Breathe in quickly, then slowly breathe out and utter *Om*.

Om …
Om …
Om …

Now, as you begin to chant the powerful *maha mrityunjaya* mantra, let your entire being focus on Lord Shiva, the primal yogi, who dwells eternally in the ultimate state of meditation and *tapasya*.

In your mind's eye, capture the picture of Lord Shiva seated on Mount Kailash, the river Bhagirati flowing from his matted locks. The sacred river was brought to this earth to grant liberation to the ancestors of King Bhagiratha. Therefore, the Bhagirati herself is a symbol of the liberation to which death is but a prelude.

Hindu philosophy teaches us that death is simply another state of being. Sunrise and sunset are nature's own rhythm. Picture the sun rising in all its glory in the eastern seas – as the sun rises here, somewhere in the far west, perhaps on the American continent, it is setting in a blaze of brilliance into the vast expanse of the western seas. As the sun sets in one continent, it is rising in another. Therefore, death upon this earth plane is a birth into another.

So many of us are afraid of death. We forget that birth and death are but two sides of the same coin. Wherever there is birth, there is bound to be death. Whoever is born must die. Leaving the body is called death, even as entering the body is called birth. Death applies only to the physical body. When the body drops down or dies, *we* do not die. We are immortal, eternal and deathless. It is the body that dies.

worthy of His children! This is what the *abhyaroha* mantra teaches us to aspire to.

It must be mentioned that this ancient prayer has been adapted to their faith by several Buddhists and Christians, thereby emphasizing the universality of our *sanatana* dharma!

The Saint and the Thief

There was a saint who lived in a small hut. The hut had a door without a latch or lock. It only had a bolt on either side of the door. Whenever the saint went out, he just bolted the door from outside. People who visited him would see the bolt and would know that the saint had gone out. The saint used to go deep into the forest during the night. To saints, the night is very precious, for it is during the night that they commune with God. It is during the night that they receive messages from the other world. It is during the night that the saints and men of God are wakeful, even while in meditation.

Every time this saint went out at night, he would merely bolt the door from outside. One night, a thief arrived on the scene; lifting the bolt, he entered the saint's *kutiya*. He gathered all the belongings of the saint and tying them together in a cloth, he carried it to the door. Alas! The bolt of the door on the outside had slipped down into the hole in the mud and the door could not be opened. The thief tried hard to open the door but in vain. Seeing a window in a wall of the *kutiya,* he jumped out through it. Then he came to the front door and tried to push the bolt open so that he could enter the *kutiya* and collect his loot. But the door would not open, for the bolt inside had slipped down thus locking the door from inside. The thief went back to the window, jumped in

A Mantra for Lord Vishnu's Grace

Om Namo Bhagavate Vasudevaya…

I prostrate myself before Lord Vasudeva, the Indweller in all…

This mantra offers salutations and asserts our surrender to Lord Vishnu, He whom we worship as Lord Rama, Lord Narayana, Lord Krishna and Lord Narasimha. His Names are countless and each one of them is sweeter than the nectar of immortality, amrita. Call Him by any Name. Call for His Grace and He will be with you, for He has given His promise to us in the *Gita*:

> *Renouncing all rites and writ duties, come unto Me alone for Single refuge: do not fear, for I shall Liberate you from all sin and suffering.*

You may be assured that the promise was not lightly made! Call Him by any one of His 1008 names! He is *Achyuta,* One who is ever stable, immovable and imperishable; He is *Ananta,* the One who is infinite and endless; He is *Madhava,* beloved of Lakshmi and the One who can help us master our minds; He is *Govinda,* the Lord who lived among us as a cowherd for our salvation; He is *Damodara,* the One who is compassionate even to the most sinful among us; He is *Narayana*, the One who is the source, abode and the goal of all beings; each of His names is a shield, a weapon against sin, evil and negative forces!

Om Namo Bhagavate Vasudevaya!

The *Srimad Bhagavatam* opens with this invocation to Vasudeva, the Cosmic Creator.

"He from whom the creation, sustenance and dissolution of this world (appear to take place); he who seems to be the material and efficient cause of it; he who is omniscient and self-effulgent; he who revealed to Brahma the *Vedas* making him the *adikavi* (the first and the foremost poet); the wisdom of which (of *Vedas*) makes the scholars wonderstruck; he upon whom this *trigunatmika* (of the three *Gunaas*) world caused by the fusion of fire, water and earth is superimposed; who by His own light of Consciousness always destroys the ignorance of maya; that Supreme Truth I meditate upon."

Maharishi Narad was dearly beloved of Vasudeva. On his lips was the Name of the Lord – constant, ever present and ever-beloved. For Narada, *Om Namo Narayana* was the mantra of his life and his soul. In this prophetic vision, the great sage foresaw the state of the world, the plight of human beings in *Kali Yuga* and knew in his wisdom that the Lord's Name would be our one great means of salvation in this age. He had converted his very *prana*, breath, into the Name Divine. Indeed, it was fitting then that he should be the one to give us the sacred *maha* mantra, which sustains so many of us amid our afflictions and ailments, physical and spiritual.

What are the benefits of chanting the Name of Narayana, Vasudeva as he is called?

Our lives are stained by evil and we hide those patches of darkness by wearing masks of pretence.

God is Truth and if you want to get closer to God, then you should bear witness to the Truth in your daily deeds.

POSITIVE VISUALIZATION

Close your eyes and meditate in silence for a minute.

Begin by chanting the mantra softly. Let its pure vibrations fill your consciousness. Continue chanting softly, untill you are filled with the peace and serenity that this mantra brings with it.

... Asatoma sat gamaya ...

The world is transient; everything in it, everything we desire, all that we crave is made up of transient shadows: they are *asat.* As you chant, consciously try to shake off the bonds that shackle you to the unreal, and become aware that there are higher things in this human life that we can all aspire to. Feel your consciousness rising higher and higher...

Tamaso ma jyotir gamaya ...

Ignorance, unawareness and lack of conscious intelligence constitute the worst darkness. Physical darkness is nothing to be afraid of! But *avidya, ajnana,* ignorance of the Supreme Truth and the truth of your own self are the equivalent of spiritual blindness. Therefore, imagine the veil of darkness being lifted and cast aside as you chant this line. Feel and see with your inner vision, the light permeating your consciousness. Feel the radiance that fills your heart. See yourself emerging, as from a dark tunnel, into the blessed warmth and light of the sunshine. Feel your world being

na krodho na cha maatsaryam na lobho na
ashubhaa matih
bhavanti krita punyaanaam bhaktaanaam
purushhottame

> Neither anger nor jealousy; neither avarice nor unholy thoughts taint the minds of the true devotees of Purushottama, who have to their credit many virtuous deeds.

Therefore, I urge you with all the persuasive power in my capacity, to let the Name Divine be on your lips constantly, as it was on Maharishi Narada's. Though there are other means to train and focus the mind, the repetition of the Name Divine is the simplest, surest and most effective way for all of us. We find it increasingly difficult to concentrate and prevent the mind from wandering of its own accord, even when we valiantly try to meditate. But chanting or singing the Name Divine focuses our wandering mind, just as a magnet draws iron filings. When we form *kirtan* groups and sing the Name Divine in chorus, we veritably create a paradise on earth, and even the most weak-willed among us will find that they are losing themselves in the ocean of nectar that is *Naam smaran*. Let *kirtan* become a habit for us, and let it pave the way Godward for us.

The Alwar saints too, for their part, have extolled the grace and benign power of the *Narayana Divya Naama* in countless verses. It gives us our identity as devotees of the Lord and brings meaning and purpose to this life; it nullifies and neutralizes all the suffering associated with this human birth; it offers us liberation from the cycle of birth and death; it is the mantra of goodness, welfare and all grace. It is the Name held out as the Supreme One in the four *Vedas*; it is

Question: *It is said different* japa malas *have different properties. How does one know which* mala *to use?*
Answer: It all depends on your mind. Choose one which appeals to you.

Question: *If we are chanting the* maha mrityunjaya *mantra for someone's health, does it mean that we are taking on their karma?*
Answer: No. By reciting the mantra, you are only offering your prayers for his speedy recovery. I do not think any selfless prayer can bring another's karma on to you.

Question: *Can one recite two different mantras in the same day?*
Answer: Yes. You can repeat as many mantras as you like. But it is always better for a beginner to concentrate on a single mantra.

The *Pranava* Mantra

Om

Omkara *(pranava)* is considered to be the sound incarnation of the Supreme Being. It symbolizes *Brahman,* the Supreme Lord. It is without beginning, it is changeless, supreme and free from any external contamination. The *Narada-pancharatra* states: "When the transcendental sound vibration is practiced by a conditioned soul, the Supreme Lord is present in this utterance." The *Atharva Veda* and the *Mandukya Upanishad* also mention the importance of *omkara. Omkara* is said to be the beginning, middle and end. It is eternal and beyond all material restrictions or contaminations.

The Lord refers to this sacred syllable in the *Gita*:

Maharshinaam bhrigur aham
giraam asmy ekam aksharam
yajnaanaam japa-yajno asmi
sthavaraanaam himalayah

[*Gita*: x – 25]

Of the great sages, I am Bhrigu; of vibrations, I am the transcendental Om. Of sacrifices, I am *japa,* the

The Story of Dhruva

Dhruva was the eldest son of a king. As the eldest, he should have been the closest to his father's heart and next in line to the throne. But the child was destined for a greater life!

Dhruva's father had two wives. Suniti, the older one, was gentle, mild and virtuous. She was Dhruva's mother. Suruchi, the younger one, was beautiful and the king's favourite. She had a son called Uttama.

One day, the two princes were playing together. Suddenly, Dhruva wanted to go and sit on the lap of his father, the king. The little boy ran up to his father who was seated on the throne, and climbed joyfully onto his knees. The king, too, embraced his little son gladly and lovingly stroked his hair.

Queen Suruchi just happened to witness this little moment. Being a proud and arrogant woman, she was incensed to see Dhruva on the king's knees. She rudely pulled the little boy by the ear and pushed him away. "Get out!" she screamed in rage. "You have no right to be seated here, on your father's lap or on his throne! That is a position meant for my son alone!" The king, who was infatuated with his younger wife, said not a word in defence of his son.

Dhruva ran to his mother. "How is it that my father's lap is not for me?" he questioned her in anguish. "Tell me how I may obtain his love, so that no one can push me away from my rightful place."

Suniti was a pious and devoted woman, as well as a loving mother. She said to her son, "My dear child, look not to your earthly father or earthly mother for comfort. Turn instead to your Divine Father; for He alone has the power to grant you your heart's desire."

Dhruva's heart was moved by his mother's words of wisdom. He went into the *tapoban* (a forest of meditation), in order to find God through the practice of austerity and devotion. As luck would have it, Maharishi Narada came to meet him there. "Tell me of the Lord who can grant me my heart's desire," the child asked the sage. In love and kindness, Maharishi Narada described the effulgent and radiant form of the four-armed Maha Vishnu with eyes as brilliant as the sun, the sacred *shank* and *chakra* in his hands, the mace and the sword at his sides, His Divine presence inspiring awe and ecstasy simultaneously. Once this form was clearly etched into Dhruva's mind, Maharishi Narada taught him the sacred mantra, *Om Namo Bhagavate Vasudevaya,* and thus, young Dhruva was initiated into meditation.

For Dhruva, it became the *taraka* mantra that would enable him to have a *darshan* of the Lord: *Om Namo Bhagavate Vasudevaya*! (I offer salutation to the Lord who is the All-Pervading One!)

For days, this five-year-old child sat in meditation of the Lord. Hunger, thirst and all bodily demands were laid aside. As he uttered the *taraka* mantra repeatedly, his consciousness was uplifted and the Lord appeared to give him *darshan.*

Dhruva had left the palace with a longing to take his rightful place on the throne and hopeful that he would one the *pranava* mantra, or that which pervades life and runs through our *prana* or breath.

I have said repeatedly, that though *Kali Yuga* is one of the toughest and most strife-ridden of the ages, it is also an age in which God has made it easy for His *bhaktas* to reach Him. Therefore, it is a sign of the times that this mantra, which was once held to be esoteric and mysterious and the prerogative of the learned few, has now become part of the daily life and routine of all believers. Most pious Hindus begin their day, their work and their travel with the chanting of this mantra. It is part of their recited and silent prayers; it is part of their pooja and *aarti.* Our students write this syllable at the very beginning of their examinations! Women wear the sacred symbol as a protective pendant, while men engrave it on their rings and so on. In many families, the sacred syllable is written on the tongue of the newborn child during its naming ceremony.

Scholars say that this sacred syllable is made up of three vital sounds: *aa, oo* and *ma.* This is why it is sometimes represented as *Aum* in English transliteration. It is also thought to be the primal sound that existed before creation, and the ultimate sound that will continue to exist after the dissolution of the Universe in the *pralaya.* It is therefore worshipped as the *naatharupa* – the sound Form of the Supreme. Our great sages, rishis and yogis have meditated on this mantra as the path to Eternal Bliss and union with the *nirguna Brahman* or Formless Nameless God. These three sounds *A–U–M* are thought to represent the Holy Trinity of Creation, Preservation and Destruction. Thus, the chanting of the mantra is a prayer or worship in itself.

fire. The heat of the fire is engulfing you but Lord Narayana is not afar.

The Name Divine is being repeated in the background of your mind.

Know that Lord Narayana will save you from the fire and that He will never desert you. He is the All Powerful! He is Eternal! He is the Protector, the Healer and the Guardian of your soul!

Now visualize the fires being doused and dying out under His benign eyes. He has saved you and you are safe in His Eternal Arms.

Lord Narayana is the Divine Protector and the great Deliverer of our souls. Carry this in your consciousness and let the chanting go on!

FREQUENTLY ASKED QUESTIONS (FAQS)

Question: *Is it necessary to do mantra* japa *during meditation?*
Answer: Mantra *japa* is in itself a form of meditation.

Question: *It is said that there are mantras that can cause harm to others. What would you say about people who practice such mantras?*
Answer: To do so is against the spirit of the scriptures and the mantras themselves!

If someone tries to practice black magic by using a mantra, it can be stopped by a person who is repeating a genuine mantra for his own protection. In this case, the harmful mantra rebounds on the one who uttered it with evil intentions. Mantras are meant to protect and bless those who utter them; they must not be used to harm others.

Lord Brahma, Lord Shiva, Kartikeya and the *Pranava* Mantra

It is said that Lord Brahma once came to Kailash to pay his respects to Lord Shiva. As he entered Lord Shiva's abode, he was accosted by the young and precocious Lord Kartikeya, who demanded to be told who He was.

Taken aback, Lord Brahma informed the lad that He was none other than the great Creator among the Holy Trinity.

"So you are the Creator of the Universe," nodded Kartikeya. "Then surely you must be able to tell me the meaning of *Aum*, the *pranava* mantra."

Lord Brahma was nonplussed, but fortunately for Him, Lord Shiva Himself arrived on the scene, amused at the confrontation between His son and their Divine Visitor.

"So what's going on here?" the Lord demanded of His younger son.

"Nothing much," said Kartikeya with mock solemnity. "He says He is the Creator of the Universe, but He has not even answered the simple question I had put to Him."

"And what might that question be, if I may be so bold as to ask?" said Lord Shiva in the same playful spirit.

"Oh, I only asked Him to tell me the meaning of *Aum*, the *Pranava* mantra."

"I see! So you asked Him to tell you the meaning! Do you know the meaning of the *pranava* mantra yourself?"

"But of course I do! Otherwise, how could I ask Him?"

"Perhaps, you will be so kind as to tell me the same?"

"With great pleasure! Shall I begin?"

"Go on, I'm listening!"

"But my dear Father," said Kartikeya, "one does not receive a mantra in this manner – with me seated down here and you towering above me in your magnificent stature! You must be like a proper disciple with folded hands, a bowed head, seated at my feet and eager to listen to my *upadesh*. For if I were to tell you the meaning of the *pranava* mantra, would I not be your Guru?"

The Lord graciously acceded to this request. He assumed the posture of the disciple before his son, while the youngster whispered the significance of the *pranava* mantra into His ears.

To this day, Kartikeya is worshipped as Lord Shiva's Preceptor in Swami-malai, a famous South Indian shrine.

POSITIVE VISUALIZATION

You must enter into the silence within, before you begin with the chanting of the *pranava* mantra.

This is a chant on the Formless Divine. It is a chant that takes you close to pure consciousness.

Sit in a relaxed posture, focus on your breath. As you breathe in and breathe out, gently chant *Om*.

philosophy. The Ganga that flows from His head symbolizes the eternal stream of *bhakti,* while His contemplative posture symbolizes the principles of *jnana* (true knowledge) and *dhyana* (meditation upon the Ultimate Truth). His ash-smeared form symbolizes the principle of *vairagya* or the detachment from worldly attractions. But let me also add, that when Lord Shiva realized that aspersions were being cast not only on his appearance but also on His beloved consort for losing her heart to Him, He took up the form of *Kalyana Sundaram* – the handsome bridegroom, in all splendour and finery. He did this so that the world would know that Goddess Parvati was the chosen bride of a much sought-after bachelor!

Scholars trace the origin of the word *Shiva* (meaning auspicious) to its first appearance in the Vedic prayer to *Rudra,* which is found in the *Yajur Veda*. This ancient hymn enumerates the auspicious and benign aspects and attributes of Lord Shiva.

Some scholars divide the five sacred syllables to indicate that the five sounds relate to our five *koshas* – the *annamaya kosha,* the *pranamaya kosha,* the *manonmaya kosha,* the *vignanamaya kosha* and the *anandamaya kosha*. The one mentioned last refers to the consciousness of the blissful self, where Shiva is said to dwell, and it is worn like a garment on our being that can give rise to this state of bliss.

Let me explain further. As human beings, the physical body, our outer form of matter, is worn like a garment on our being. This is the *annamaya kosha*. Within this outer sheath is the *prana* or vital breath, which constitutes the *pranamaya kosha;* our mind, or the instrument of cognition, constitutes the *manonmaya kosha*; the ego and the intellect together constitute our *vignanamaya kosha;* and the consciousness of pure bliss, which is the innermost sheath, is the *anandamaya kosha* – folded in the centre of the five sheaths resides the true self – that which is. Caught up as we are in the mire of worldly existence, most of us rarely experience this bliss, or indeed become aware of our true self.

The *Puranas* provide a beautiful narrative to help us understand this complex idea. It is said that Goddess Shakti, the principle of Divine energy, created this world in all its changeable manifestations and invited Her celestial partner Lord Shiva to come and dwell with Her in the world she had created. Lord Shiva told Her that He represented the principle of unchangeable, stable and permanent reality; how then, could He dwell in Her constantly changing world? Goddess Shakti then pointed out to him that if He came to dwell at the very centre of Being, which was ever-fixed and centred in *ananda,* that centre would take on his unchangeability and would remain ever constant, ever the same. Everything around Him would change, but He would remain the *sat chit ananda* – the unchanging bliss at the centre of all Consciousness. Therefore, Lord Shiva is described as the true Self that resides in us all; and the sacred *Namah Shivaya* mantra is the link to our true self of bliss and truth!

I am sure that many of my readers are familiar with these unforgettable lines:

Mano Buddhi Ahankara Chitta Ninaham
Nacha Shrotra Jihve Na Cha Ghrana Netre
Nacha Vyoma Bhoomir Na Tejo Na Vayu
Chidananda Rupah Shivoham Shivoham

The *Gita's* Mantra

Om tat sat

Om tat sad iti nirdeso
brahmanas tri-vidhah smrtah
brahmanaas tena vedaas ca
yajnaas ca vihitaah puraa

From the beginning of creation, the three syllables – *om tat* and *sat* – have been used to indicate the Supreme Absolute Truth [*Brahman*]. They were uttered by brahmanas while chanting Vedic hymns and during sacrifices for the satisfaction of the Supreme.

[***Gita*, XVII- 23**]

O*m tat sat* is recognized by the great *jnanis* and the *bhaktas* as the three-fold manifestation of the Supreme *Brahman,* the transcendent *Paramatman* (supreme spirit) that pervades all existence. The *Taitiriya Upanishad* states: *Om iti brahman om iti sarvam* [I:VIII:I]. This means that *Om* is synonymous with the *Brahman. Om* is understood to be the spiritual substance of existence. *Om* is the transcendental sound vibration chanted before commencing every Vedic

If we are fortunate and the grace of God is upon us, a day comes in our lives when we see the futility of all the running around and the restlessness. Our soul is awakened and we realize that we have wandered far too long. The truth dawns on us that we have dwelt in darkness till now and the restlessness will give way to an overwhelming sense of emptiness within. Our heart longs for peace and we are filled with a sense of yearning to realize the goal of our life.

Om Namah Shivaya is not only a powerful mantra that can help us realize this goal, it is also a mantra that can be chanted for cleansing our inner *koshas* and can help us connect with our innermost self. It is said that reciting this mantra can free us from the necessity to perform rites and rituals, for as this mantra begins to vibrate in our consciousness, we effortlessly attain oneness with the divine that is within us.

This popular mantra is chanted in various well-known forms: *Namah Shivaya, Namaha Shiva, Shivaya Shiva, Shivaya Namah,* and perhaps the most often recited and chanted in *kirtan* among the youth today *Shiva Shambo!*

to us in the *Gita* – God pervades the whole Universe; all things are rooted in Him, but He is not rooted in them. He transcends the Universe. He is the Eternal, universal Atman that pervades creation. By fixing our minds on Him and worshipping Him, we can reach Him. He is the Transcendent and Immanent one. He alone abides.

Those who have read the *Gita* with attention and devotion will know that each chapter ends with these words:

Om tatsaditi srimad bhagavad gitasu upanishatsu brahmavidyaayaam
yogashaastre srikrishna arjuna samvaade sankhya yogo naama dvitiyo'dhyaayah.

[End of Ch.II]

Thus, with the words, *Om, Tat, Sat* — the names of the Lord as sung by the Lord Himself in the *Upanisad* of the *Bhagavad Gita*, the science of *Brahma*, the scripture on yoga, the dialogue between Lord Krishna and Arjuna, the second chapter entitled, '*Sankhyaa Yoga*' ends.

Om, Tat, Sat has been declared by Lord Krishna Himself, as the triple designation of the Absolute. These three names are pronounced as a benediction at the end of each chapter by Sage Veda Vyasa himself. For the Lord assures us, these three syllables can wash away the mistakes that we might have committed in pronouncing the verses, words and letters in the chapter. So, these three words are pronounced at the end of each chapter.

Brahman Satyam, Jagath Mithyam. "The self is real and the world is illusory," Adi Shankara declared. Similarly, he asserted

Sarvam Vishnumayam Jagath – "The Universe is permeated by God". When scholars pointed out the contradiction in his statements, Shankara explained the difference between permanence and impermanence: Worldly life is continually changing and moving, like moving scenes on a permanent screen. In this process, the world and the Divine are one, but the world is perishable, changeable and impermanent, while the Divine is Eternal and Unchangeable.

The awareness of this separation from Her beloved brought tears to Her eyes and She wept, repenting Her actions. She realized that the honour, the praise and the gifts bestowed on Her had led Her away from Her beloved. She wanted to go back to Him, but She had wandered so far that She could not find Her way back to Mount Kailash. As Her eyes overflowed with tears, She cried out to Lord Shiva, "O my Lord, You are ever so kind, You always hear the call of your devotees, You have always protected and taken care of them. O Lord, I pine for you. I do not want to live away from you even for a moment, I want to return home and be at your Lotus Feet."

Interestingly, one version of the legend states that it was Maharishi Narada who taught Her the power and efficacy of the mantra, *Om Namah Shivaya.*

And forthwith, She took up the chanting of the sacred *panchakshara* mantra.

Lord Shiva, a devotee of devotees, heard Her heartbroken cry and instantly appeared before Her. "I have come to take you back home," He said to Her graciously. To this day, people worship Lord Shiva and Goddess Parvati at the sacred spot where He came to take Her back home with Him. A beautiful temple dedicated to this event in the *Shiv Purana* exists there, commemorating the Lord's grace and kindness to His devotees.

POSITIVE VISUALIZATION

Om Namah Shivaya is the chant that can take us to the highest crest of spirituality that can be attained within each one of us. As you sit in silence with your eyes closed and breathe rhythmically, keep repeating the mantra, *Om Namah Shivaya.*

Begin to visualize that you are on the snowy mountains of Kailash. Imagine that endless silence, peace and tranquility surround you. Here, everything is still and eternal; it is timeless, having no beginning or end. Nothing matters but stillness and nothingness.

Shivoham! Shivoham! That is what you are! Pure light and pure consciousness is what you have come to experience! *Om Namah Shivaya!*

Allow your consciousness to rise higher and higher as you chant the mantra.

Become aware that you are not the ego or the intellect; you are not restricted to the five senses; there is no reason for you to be limited by likes and dislikes, joy and sorrow; life and death need not hold any fear for you, for you are not a narrow, small, limited creature! You are That! *Tat twam asi!*

Shivoham! Shivoham! You are pure consciousness and pure bliss!

Dwell in this awareness as long as you can. Let the chant go on!

FREQUENTLY ASKED QUESTIONS (FAQS)

Question: *Is the use of a* Japa mala *necessary to chant the mantra*?

Answer: No. There are teachers who will teach you how to count the beads on the knuckles of your fingers. The *Japa mala* is useful only to those who are habituated to it, but it is not essential.

Question: *Does initiation take place only by a mantra given by the Guru or are there other ways of initiation?*

The rustic did as he was told. Nidagha got on his shoulders and said: "Know it now. I am above as the king and you are below as the elephant. Is that clear enough?"

"No, not yet," was the rustic's gentle reply. "You say you are above like the king and I am below like the elephant. The 'king', the 'elephant', 'above' and 'below' – so far that is clear. But pray, tell me, what do you mean by 'I' and 'you'?"

When Nidagha was suddenly confronted with the mighty problem of distinguishing a 'you' from an 'I', light dawned in his mind. At once, he jumped down and fell at his master's feet saying, "Who else but my venerable Master Ribhu could have thus drawn my mind from the superficialities of physical existence to the true Being of the Self? Oh! Gracious Master, I crave thy blessings!"

"Understand, dear Nidagha," said the Sage, "when one is convinced that he is always That which is *Sat-chit-ananda* (Existence-Consciousness-Bliss) and abides by That in a state of complete identity, he casts off the unreal bondage of identification with birth and death and attains liberation. Therefore, one attains purity of mind by constantly thinking that everything known is the Supreme Being and that the Supreme Being is oneself. Thereafter, by abiding in the state of complete identity with the Absolute Reality, liberation can be attained here and now. I have spoken the truth, *Om Tat Sat*!"

POSITIVE VISUALIZATION

Start with the mental chanting of the mantra *Om*. Breathe slowly and concentrate deeply on the incoming breath, feeling its freshness and coolness. With the outgoing breath, chant *Tat Sat,* feeling the warmth.

The Sacred Mantra of *Rama Naam*

We have already seen the power and the efficacy of the *maha* mantra. Some of you might therefore wonder why it is necessary to take up the *Rama Naam* separately once again. After all, you might argue, that we have all along stressed that Lord Rama and Lord Krishna are One.

Let me remind you of a nursery rhyme which many of us are familiar with:

If all the world were paper,
And all the seas were ink,
If all the trees were bread and cheese,
What should we do for drink?

My dear friends, if all the world and the skies and this vast universe were paper, if all the seas and rivers and rain were ink, and all of us humans wrote whatever we could about the glory of the *Rama Naam* using this inexhaustible source of ink and paper – we would still do scant justice to the *Rama Naam mahima*!

In the *Vishnu Sahasranama* we have a verse in which Goddess Parvati humbly requests Lord Shiva to teach her

even get them tattooed on their arms. What are your views on this?
Answer: Whatever we do, we should always have respect for the mantra. It should not be treated lightly.

Question: *In* Kriya Yoga, *a mantra is combined with yoga. Is this combination advisable?*
Answer: A mantra can be combined with yoga, but it is always better to follow the Guru's instructions.

The *Shanti* Mantra

Om sarve bhavantu sukinah
sarve santu niraamayaah
sarve bhadrani pashyantu
maa kaschit dhukha bhaag bhavet
Om shaantih shaantih shaantih

OM, may all be happy
May all be free from disabilities
May all see the good of others
May none be in misery
OM, Peace, Peace, Peace!

It is in the glorious tradition of the *Vedas* to offer universal prayers for the benefit of all humanity, indeed, all of creation. Selfish needs and personal desires are secondary to universal welfare and humanitarian concerns. In this sacred scripture, the concept of *vasudhaiva kutumbakam* is given: all the Universe is One Family of the Supreme Lord.

Our great sages and saints believed in the idea that the only prayer worth uttering was the prayer for the good of all – that is, a prayer for others rather than ourselves. This concept finds its most beautiful expression in this mantra.

I urge you to take note of the term repeated throughout

mantras are put together to form the *taraka* mantra of *Rama Naam!* One might be tempted to conclude this ingenious explication with the Pythogorean proof of proposition: QED. Thus Proved!

Whenever our freedom fighters faced frustration or lack of progress in their quest for independence, Mahatma Gandhi would energize his followers by making them chant the *Rama Naam* with him. As we know, none of his meetings ever concluded without the *Rama dhuni.* In fact, the Father of the Nation died with the name of Lord Rama upon his lips.

I might add that the devout of this land believe that Lord Kashi Vishwanath takes upon Himself the onerous task of initiating the uninitiated at the point of death, by whispering the sacred *Rama Naam* into the ears of all devout Hindus, even as they breathe their last breath on this earth! In His infinite compassion, the Lord does this to ensure our salvation even at the eleventh hour!

In South India, the *Rama Naam* is practiced in both oral and written forms *(likhit japa)* by countless devotees. The mantra in its written form is offered by millions upon millions of these people at the sacred feet of their Gurus and acharyas. *Malas* (garlands) made of little pieces of paper, each of them bearing the *Rama Naam,* are offered to Lord Hanuman who lived, breathed and personified *Rama bhakti.*

Guru Nanak Dev tells us in his sacred verse, "*Vada Sahib, Vada Thao, Oonche Upar Ooncha Nao*" – The Name of God is the Alpha, the highest. There is nothing higher than that. Therefore, say the Name Divine with every bead and every breath of your life. Blessed is the man who understands the divinity of the word Rama. Such a man lives in the world but is ever in the presence of the Divine. He never ever forgets the Name Divine. The chanting of the sacred word goes on within his heart. The Name of Rama is so sacred that by chanting it man can overcome his destiny!

The Name of Lord Rama is exalted by saints and sages alike. The sacred *Guru Granth Sahib* venerates the Name of Lord Rama, and so does *Kabir Granth*. Gurudev Sadhu Vaswani also venerated the Name of Lord Rama in the *Nuri Granth*. It would be no exaggeration to say that the Name of Lord Rama is inscribed on the soul of India.

we grow in the spirit of fellowship and understanding," say our ancient Hindu scriptures. And the *Rig Veda*, perhaps the oldest of all scriptures, says: "Together walk ye, and together talk ye and together know ye your minds!"

I believe that the world is the garden of God. He is in all that is – men and women, birds and animals, fish and fowl, worms and insects, trees and flowers, rivers and rocks, stones and stars, and even in this pen that scribbles and the paper on which my moving fingers write, "Krishna! Krishna!" Lord Krishna is in all, and we all are in Lord Krishna! When we have this vision of the One-in-all and All-in-one, we will grow in the spirit of Brotherhood of all creation!

One day, I was out on a walk with a few of my friends. A man brushed past us, walking in a hurry. Even though our eyes met for only a second, I folded my hands in greeting. The man was under such stress that he continued on his way without a response.

One of my friends said to me, "Dada, you greeted him with a *namaste* and he did not even return your greeting!"

My reply was, "I fold my hands only to pay obeisance to the God who resides within everyone and not to greet the outer form!"

Is not this the vision of the One-in-all given to us in the *Vedas*? Lord Krishna tells us the same thing in His song Divine, the *Bhagavad Gita*:

Who sees Me
Deathlessly dwelling
In all that is,
And who sees All in Me –
Of him I shall not lose hold
Nor shall he lose hold of Me!

the help of Maharishi Narada. Naradmuni, as we all know, is the one who creates all the riddles and enigmas and he is also the one who solves them. Naradmuni said to Lord Ganesha, "It does not matter. Just write the word *Rama* and then circle around it. The entire universe is encompassed in the word *Rama*." Lord Ganesha did so and was the first one to go back to Lord Brahma.

Lord Brahma was amazed. He asked Ganesha, "Did you not travel around the universe?" Lord Ganesha replied, "I did indeed, Lord, I have returned only after having done what you asked."

"But so soon... ?" Lord Brahma hesitated in disbelief.

Lord Ganesha then spoke of writing the word *Rama* and how he then circumambulated it, being aware that the entire universe was contained in its meaning. Lord Brahma was delighted and pleased. He accepted Lord Ganesha's argument and declared Him the Superior Deity of them all. That is why Lord Ganesha is known as Ganapati – the Leader of the Deities. He is also considered a good omen, which will enable us to overcome the most difficult obstacles and accomplish near-impossible tasks. Even today, every pooja offered in our homes and temples begins with the praise of Lord Ganesha. He knew the greatness of the word *Rama*!

There are many instances of miracles performed with the word *Rama*. Let me tell you about one from the life of Sant Kabir. Once, a leper-beggar went to his house to get his blessings. Sant Kabir was not at home at that time. The leper knocked on the door and asked Kabir's wife Loi, "Where is Sant Kabir?"

Loi asked the leper, "What is your problem?" to which the leper replied, "I am suffering from the deadly disease of

We work for no reward:
We help the poor and needy
For love of Him, our Lord!

We're friends of all the friendless,
Servers of those in pain!
We're brothers of the voiceless,
The cow, the dog, the hen!

We trust in God, His mercy,
And in ourselves believe:
All what today we hope for
We shall one day achieve!

Hand in hand we march on still:
A better world to build,
A world of love and laughter,
With peace and plenty filled!

I have always asserted that Hinduism is not a religion, but a way of life. The Hindu way of life embraces all of God's creation in its entirety! For *Vedanta* teaches us that there is but One Life in all! The One Life sleeps in the mineral and the stone, stirs in the vegetable and plant, dreams in the animal and wakes up in man. Creation is one family. Therefore, let us not forget that birds and animals are also our younger brothers and sisters! It is our duty to guard them and protect them!

My vision of fellowship and brotherhood shows me a world in which the right to life is accorded to every creature that breathes the breath of life! How can wars cease until we put an end to all killing? How can we claim to seek world peace, when we continue to slaughter sentient creatures? For if a man kills an animal for food, he will not hesitate in killing a fellow man whom he regards as an enemy! Therefore, I urge you to let us grow in the true spirit of brotherhood. Let us grow in the spirit of Reverence for all Life!

In this regard, I would like to offer you a practical suggestion; it is a very simple suggestion. Everyday, breathe out this simple prayer at least five times:

> *May all living beings be happy, full of peace and bliss; may those that are in the north and those that are in the south, may those that are in the east and those that are in the west, those that are tall, those that are tiny, those that are rich, those that are poor, those that are young, those that are old, those that are educated, those that are illiterate, those that are born, those that are yet in the womb unborn, may all be happy and full of peace and bliss.*

Offer this prayer once after getting up, once before breakfast, once before lunch, once before dinner and once before you retire for the night.

Let us go a step further:

> *May those that love me and those who, for some reason or other, are unable to love me, may they all be happy, full of peace and bliss. May those that speak well of me and those that, for some reason or other, are unable to speak well of me, may they all be happy, full of peace and bliss. May all be happy! May all be at peace!*

Let the whole world vibrate with your radiations of peace and you will bring peace on earth. The more you radiate peace, the more you pave the way for peace!

Question: *It is said that a mantra should be chanted or meditated upon only after a bath and at certain times of day. How true is this?*
Answer: Except when indicated by the Guru, there are no restrictions on chanting or meditating upon a mantra.

Question: *When does a Guru know that his disciple is ready for the mantra?*
Answer: When the Guru feels that the disciple's ego has been annihilated and the disciple is in complete harmony with the Guru – such a disciple is then ready to receive the *Guru* mantra.

Question: *Is it possible for the disciple to ask the Guru to change the mantra if not much progress is being made?*
Answer: The disciple should feel free to place all his difficulties before the Guru in order to resolve the problems that vex him.

The *Abhyaroha* Mantra

Om Asato Maa Sadgamaya
Tamaso Maa Jyotirgamaya
Mrityormaa Amritam Gamaya
Om Shaantih Shaantih Shaantih

From the unreal (the non-existent, the apparent), lead me to the real;
From darkness (of ignorance), lead me to the Light (of wisdom);
From death, lead me to eternal life.

These words which are familiar to most of us, first occur in the *Brihadaranyaka Upanishad,* and constitute what is known as the *abhyaroha* mantra – the mantra which can raise our consciousness. *Aaroha* literally means 'ascent'. This invocation, too, can take us onward, upward and Godward. This mantra is at once a prayer, a chant and an invocation to the Divine. In the original text, it is repeated continuously to produce the required effect – freedom from falsehood and the darkness of ignorance. The three lines of this verse are also known as the *pavamana* mantras or purifying chants. It is thought that they can help the true seeker rise from the mortal to the immortal level where his atman truly belongs.

would liberate his soul. And not once, not twice, but 18 times, the master sent him away, empty-handed. We are told that Lord Vishnu himself urged the Guru, through a message, to impart the Divine mantra to Sri Ramanuja; however, the Guru was determined to follow the letter and spirit of the law which stipulated: "Reveal not the high truths except to those who have been through a year's austere apprenticeship," – that is, those who are serious, dutiful, committed and devoted to God.

And so, Ramanuja travelled 18 times to the Guru's place, and 18 times he received an indifferent response: "Not this time; go away now, and come again some other day."

The Guru had only one idea: to test Ramanuja's faith and zeal and to ensure that his spirit was strong and capable of rising above the lower passions. Finally, moved by Ramanuja's exemplary spirit, the Guru revealed the sacred mantra to him, which was, at that time, occult and hidden from all humanity, and which we now refer to as the sacred *Ashtakshara* or eight-syllabled mantra – *Om Namo Narayana*.

Gosthi Purna cautioned Ramanuja that the mantra was to be kept secret from all. He warned Ramanuja that if he should ever utter the secret mantra to another, he would go to hell. "Ramanuja! Keep this powerful mantra a secret, for all who repeat this mantra will attain salvation. Give it only to worthy disciples!"

What followed this initiation is well documented in the Acharya's life and in all *Vaishnava* historical records. Ramanuja was compassion incarnate. His love for the masses of *jivatmas* struggling in the Ocean of Samsara was truly unbounded. Why should these ordinary, humble people be denied the chance for liberation? Should it not the knowledge of who I am, what my nature really is and the truth of my human existence. This is the greatest truth we all need to learn: I am not this body that I wear; I am the immortal spirit within! This is the Truth, the Light, the Liberating factor this mantra refers to.

Satyan nasti paro dharma (there is no religion or duty higher than truth), proclaim India's ancient scriptures. *Satyan nasti paro dharma* was the teaching of ancient rishis. Mahatma Gandhi often said, "People say God is Truth. I believe that Truth is God!" When he was a student, they put a question to Mahatma Gandhi, "Tell us what is more precious than silver?" He answered, "Gold is more precious than silver." "Is there anything that is more precious than gold?" he was asked. "Truth is more precious than gold and there is nothing that is more precious than Truth," he answered. Gurudev Sadhu Vaswani emphasized the same when he said to us, "Truth, though she take me through the fire: Truth, though she lead me to the scaffold!"

Truth is not a feeble thing that you and I need to save and protect. Let us not underestimate the power of Truth, for our scriptures also assert *satyameva jayate*! Truth alone triumphs! And the truth that will always triumph is the knowledge of the Divine Being that is manifested in all of us, the immanence of God and the awareness that we are not just frail beings, but immortal spirits lit by the spark of His Divine fire. *Ishwarah sarvabhutanaam hriddhe Arjuna tisthathi*, Lord Krishna tells us in the *Gita*. "The Lord dwelleth in the hearts of all beings, O Arjuna!"

If we are indeed His children, made in His likeness, coming from Him and destined to return to His abode, His lotus feet, then we also need to cultivate qualities that are

POSITIVE VISUALIZATION

This is a mantra that you can chant aloud, so that its sound vibrations influence the home and the environment you live in. Chant continuously, so that its selfless benedictions and altruism affect your thinking to change your consciousness and the way you think about yourself and others.

As you continue chanting, reflect on this fact: everyone on this planet seeks happiness and escape from suffering. You are no different from your brother or your neighbour, your friends, colleagues, the men and women you transact business with, your fellow pilgrims on the journey of life, Egyptians, Jews, Arabs, Chinese, Japanese, New Zealanders or Chileans – all, without exception, long for peace and happiness!

You now begin to realize your oneness with all that is, all men, all creatures, all things, all climes and all conditions. You are not separate from others. You and the others are parts of the one great whole. You are in every man, in every woman, in every child. You are in every unit of life, in every bird, animal, fowl, fish, insect, shrub and plant. You belong to all countries and communities, all races and religions. You are at one with the Universe. As you become aware of this oneness of all creation, you find your heart filled with loving kindness and a spirit of kinship and compassion with all things, all beings in this vast and wonderful world.

As you continue chanting, feel a sense of peace enveloping you: feel the blessings and benedictions of the Supreme Being cast its healing, protecting grace on you. For your part, extend this grace and healing to all those whom you have come into contact with. Therefore, feel yourself a part of the Whole, a member of the universal family of Creation.

Continue the chanting; breathe out peace, happiness, goodwill and bliss to all. May all be happy and full of peace and bliss. Think of all who dwell in the Northern lands and pray in the heart within: "May all who dwell in the Northern lands be happy and full of peace and bliss." Then think of all who dwell in the Southern lands and offer the prayer, "May all who dwell in the Southern lands be happy and full of peace and bliss." Likewise, "May all who dwell in Eastern lands and all who dwell in Western lands, may they all be happy and full of peace and bliss."

Breathe out peace and goodwill to all. May all be happy and full of peace and bliss. All living things, whether they be near or far, big or tiny, rich or poor, educated or illiterate; whether they be born or are still in the womb unborn, may all, all be happy and full of peace and bliss. May those who love you and those who, for some reason or other, are unable to love you; may those who speak well of you, and those who, for some reason or other, are unable to speak well of you, may all, all without exception, be happy and full of peace and bliss. You are in them all. It is only when they become happy that you are happy. May all be free from disease, ignorance and sorrow.

Feel the peace that passeth, surpasseth understanding, infusing your body, mind, heart and soul. Send out these vibrations of peace to one and all!

FREQUENTLY ASKED QUESTIONS (FAQS)

Question: *Do you have to change your way of life to benefit from the chanting of mantras?*
Answer: It could also work the other way! If you chant the

and tried to open the door from the inside. As he was doing so, the bolt outside once again got stuck in the hole in the mud. He tried many times, but no amount of pushing and pulling would open the door. Every time he tried to open it from outside, the door was bolted from inside; and every time he tried to open it from inside; it was bolted from the outside. Nevertheless, the thief did not give up. He continued with his efforts to open the door throughout the night but did not succeed. He was wondering what to do, when, at the break of the dawn, the saint returned to his *kutiya,* and found the thief inside.

He gently asked the thief, "Dear one, who are you?" The thief narrated the whole story and described his futile efforts to open the door throughout the night. After hearing him out patiently, the saint told him, "You can take away whatever you like from here. But I wish to tell you one thing – I need men like you. In fact, I am in search of a man like you." Saying so, the saint embraced the thief and bestowed on him a loving glance of grace. In that one moment, the thief's heart changed. He fell at the feet of the saint, weeping, and said, "Kindly accept me at your lotus feet. I have committed many sins in my life. I have plundered houses and committed many other crimes. For all of those misdeeds, I seek your forgiveness. O, man of God, forgive me. Make me anew."

The saint replied, "I accept you, for I have always been in quest for men like you."

Let me explain to you why this man of God accepted the thief who had come to plunder his house as his disciple. First of all, the thief was honest. On being asked by the saint, he had confessed immediately that he was a thief and that his motive was to rob the saint's house. He had said this without any hesitation or any attempt at falsehood. Secondly, the thief had persisted in his efforts to open the door throughout the night. He had tried umpteen times to open the door from the inside and from the outside. He continued his efforts, throughout the night, even when night had turned to dawn. The saint said, "I need men who are truthful and do not give up easily, men who persevere and will continue their efforts till their goal is realized."

I hope this incident will make you reflect on the life we lead. Are we truthful? Do we live a transparent life? If we are truthful, many of us would be forced to concede that our life is full of lies and falsehood. Social psychologists talk about the games people play and the roles that they assume in their daily life: our real personality is hidden from the world. We wear a mask of goodness, we dress well and perfume our bodies and pose as honest and clean.

It is human nature to try to find in others what we lack. When we are untruthful, we suspect others of being the same. It is also human nature to conceal one's faults from one's self, because we are not able to face our own faults. When we are not true to ourselves, how can we be true to others? How can we be true to our Guru?

Going back to the story of the saint and the thief, the saint was highly impressed with the honesty of the thief and his ceaseless perseverance.

If only you would realize the value of these two virtues and implement them in your daily life, I assure you that your Guru will welcome you with open arms and shower His choicest blessings on you! But unfortunately, we keep the truth hidden from men of God. In the presence of holy ones, we pretend to be swans, but in reality, we are merely crows.

birth. Alas, our poor efforts are not enough to cleanse these impurities. But the Guru's grace can cleanse us and lead us towards the Divine Light of God.

The Third Eye or the Inner Eye of the Spirit remains closed for most of us, its vision impaired by our bad karma. The cataract of the ego, the veils of arrogance and pride, have covered this inner eye completely. The Guru is the eye surgeon, who can restore our inner vision.

The Guru reaches out to us, and with his grace, he annihilates the ego, tears away the veils of ignorance which shield us from self-realization and reveals our true identity to us – *Tat twam asi*! That art Thou! It is His grace that delivers us from bondage to the circle of life and death. This gift of Grace has devolved on the Guru from God Himself, for He knows that the world is in dire need of Grace. God's Presence is, of course, Universal: He gives us the Guru for our individual benefit and personal liberation. This is why our ancient scriptures enjoin us to venerate the Guru as God:

Gurur Brahma, Gurur Vishnu
Gurur Devo Maheshwarah
Guruh Saakshaat Parabrahma
Tasmai Sri Gurave Namah

> For me the Guru is Lord Brahma, Lord Vishnu and Lord Shiva. He creates, sustains knowledge and destroys the weeds of ignorance. I salute such a Guru.

In this human birth, we cannot see God in person, but it is our good fortune that we can see the Guru, hear his *upadesh*, associate ourselves with his daily *satsang*, accept his gracious *prasad* – indeed, grasp his holy feet firmly. Through Him, all of God's blessings and all of His grace will come to us!

filled with this light! Feel your consciousness rising higher and higher...

Mrityorma amritam gamaya...

You are not this changeable, perishable, vulnerable body that you wear! You are the immortal Spirit within! As you chant this line, become aware that the atman is indestructible and imperishable. Therefore, there is no such thing as death to the atman. The destination of your life is not death but the state that transcends death – eternity. It is the state of bliss that is your birthright and the state of union with your origin, which is pure Divinity! Feel that you are an aspect of this Divinity. Realize that your atman is too vast, too radiant and too brilliant to be cooped and confined by fears, insecurities and negativities! Feel your consciousness rising higher and higher...

Feel yourself enveloped in pure Light as you continue chanting.

Let the Light guide you from wrongdoing to righteousness.

Let the light take you to the great beyond which is eternal and deathless!

Let it lead you, guide you and light your way wherever you move. Carry it in your heart and soul.

FREQUENTLY ASKED QUESTIONS (FAQS)

Question: *Is repeating a mantra more powerful than saying a prayer? If so, can you explain why?*
Answer: There is no yardstick with which to measure the power of a prayer that comes from the very depths of the heart and a mantra which is uttered with deep love and devotion.

According to Sadhu Vaswani's teachings, the Guru is much more than a simple instructor or advisor. He is a dynamic person with a transforming power, for spirituality is a tremendous shakti and the true Guru is a man of this shakti. By the method of evocation, the Guru draws out the disciple's spiritual energy. Therefore, we read in the ancient texts, "The Guru leads forth the pupil to Himself!" It is in this process of 'leading forth', drawing the disciple to Himself – not in merely communicating information, that the secret of the Guru's shakti resides.

The Guru is also the great purifier. *Kama, krodha, lobh, moha* and *ahankaar* are all obstacles on the path of a spiritual aspirant. The Guru has the power to cleanse the disciple and break the tyranny of senses over the mind. The Guru above all, purifies the ego-consciousness of his pupil and helps him to dwell on the Highest.

The Guru is the true awakener, who can shake us awake from the deep slumber we are in. He is the kindly light, who can lead us away from the encircling gloom and to the Eternal Radiance, which is our true nature and our true Home.

The Guru creates us anew. We are reborn in spirit when we surrender to him. He is much more than advisor or professor. He is an enlightener with the transforming power of spirituality, a tremendous shakti. And it is with this shakti that He leads forth the disciple, not only towards liberation but also towards himself, so that the disciple becomes a teacher in his own right.

Therefore, we revere the Guru as the Light-bringer; His words of wisdom, His *bani,* charged with Divine and holy meaning, enter the heart and shine there as bright jewels; they lead the disciple to the Presence Divine. In darkness, the Guru's words act as the disciple's torch; they are the disciple's source of true happiness in this broken life that so often brings strife and despair.

Sri Desika, one of the great Vaishnava preceptors, has this to say of the Guru:

> A single glance from the Guru's eye will confer greater benefits than –
> The three eyes of Shiva;
> The eight eyes of Brahma;
> The thousand eyes of Vishnu.

God is not higher than the preceptor, adds Sri Desika. Nothing in the world can match the graciousness of the Guru's glance.

Sri Ramana Maharishi, a great saint, tells us, "God and Guru are not really different: they are identical. He that has earned the grace of the Guru shall undoubtedly be saved and never forsaken."

How true it is that God and the Guru are identical! There is no difference between the two: indeed, the Guru is our visible God!

No amount of devotion, no deed of service, no words of tribute from us can match the magnificence of the Guru's grace on us. Therefore, our ancient *Upanishads* enjoin us to have the same high devotion for the Guru, as we have for God.

Why does the Hindu way of life equate the Guru with Lord Brahma, Lord Vishnu and Lord Shiva? At one level, the answer is obvious. God is, of course, omnipresent, omnipotent and omniscient; it is true that while we are clad

chanting of the holy names, and of immovable things,
I am the Himalayas.

What else can we say about this *mool* mantra? Lord Krishna Himself explains that He is the transcendental *Om* vibration and that *japa* is the purest of *yajnas* or sacrifices that we can offer to Him.

Lord Brahma is that aspect of the Trinity who is the Creator. We could say that He was the First Being created and that Sage Brighu, the greatest among rishis, was His son. The transcendental sound *Om,* takes its place as the Prime Syllable (*Eka aksharam*), and *japa* or chanting as the primary form of sacrifice.

We may understand, therefore, that by the *japa* and the hearing of the holy sound of this mantra, indeed, even from its sacred vibrations, one can attain spiritual realization. This, in essence, is the process of mantra-yoga. Although the mantra is powerful in itself, when it is chanted with the faith and intensity of a true devotee, it acquires even more power. This effect is also achieved when a disciple is fortunate enough to be initiated by a spiritual mentor or Guru into a mantra for his spiritual progress.

As we know, all chanting of the *Vedas* or *Vedic* verses begins (and ends) with the chanting of *Om,* because *Om* is the *bija* or seed mantra at the beginning of most Vedic chants and mantras. In fact, *Om* is also used as yoga's preeminent and fundamental chant for training in *pranayama* or breath control. The aspirant or *sadhaka* is taught to chant *Om* in the process of controlling his breathing. As we know, breath control is accepted as a way of steadying, stabilizing, controlling and purifying the mind. Through repeated chanting of this mantra and the combined practice of *pranayama,* the aspirant can take the first steps towards controlling the mind and gradually turning it away from worldly desires and preoccupations to focus on self-realization, which is the way to liberation.

The *Mandukya Upanishad* states: "*Om* is the one eternal syllable of which all that exists is but the development. The past, the present and the future are all included in this one sound, and all that exists beyond the three forms of time is also implied in it."

Here is what the *Katha Upanishad* tells us about this sacred mantra:

> The goal which all the *Vedas* declare, which all austerities aim at, and which men desire when they lead the life of continence... is *Om*. This syllable *Om* is indeed *Brahman*. Whosoever knows this syllable obtains all that he desires. This is the best support; this is the highest support. Whosoever knows this support is adored in the world of Lord Brahma.

Brahman is incomprehensible to the untrained mind. In our state of physical existence, we can never ever hope to achieve this Supreme Knowledge, but the *pranava* mantra is the closest that we can attain to the cognizance of this Truth. It is a profound symbol, whose sound vibrations can help us realize this Truth, instinctively and intuitively. For those of us who worship the Unmanifest, it takes us closer to the *nirguna Brahman.* For those of us who hold the form of the *ishta devata* dear, it can bring the form of *saguna Brahman* closer to our consciousness. That is why we refer to this as is the picture of purity and selflessness. In the heart of such a person, resides the earnest desire of the well-being of all creation. The Guru is an ocean of love, and his love encompasses us all. The only thing we can do to deserve this love is to offer him complete and utter devotion!

So we face the final paradox: Guru-*bhakti* is for our lasting benefit, but the Guru stands to gain nothing by it!

Nevertheless, the good that we derive from Guru-*bhakti* is unbelievable:

- At the highest level, it confers liberation upon us – everlasting peace and joy, in union with God.
- As human beings, it helps us to cultivate the spirit of detachment and desirelessness to the extent that is possible for each one of us, thus freeing us from the bonds of *moha* and maya.
- At a lower level, constant devotion to the Guru also helps us gain control over our lower emotions, to resist dangerous temptations and to desist from wrong and sinful actions.
- In our everyday lives, Guru-*bhakti* gives us the strength to conquer fear, pessimism, despair, anxiety and negative thoughts.

The best part is that we need no special spiritual attainment to practice Guru-*bhakti* yoga! All we need is a yearning heart, an aspiring soul! Our role-models are great saints and holy men, who have conquered the Self and attained immortality through their Guru-*bhakti*. Therefore, we find ourselves in the brotherhood of evolved souls, when we start on the path of Guru-*bhakti*.

The devotion and dedication we offer to the Guru reach

In his characteristically simple and beautiful way, Sri Ramakrishna Paramahansa tells us:

> The sound *OM* is *Brahman*. The rishis and sages practiced austerity to realize that Sound. After attaining perfection, one hears the sound of this eternal Word rising spontaneously from within. 'What will you gain,' some sages ask, 'by merely hearing this sound?' You hear the roar of the ocean from a distance. By following the roar, you can reach the ocean. As long as there is the roar, there must also be the ocean. By following the trail of *OM*, you attain *Brahman*, of which the Word is the symbol. That *Brahman* has been described by the *Vedas* as the ultimate goal. The *sandhya* merges in the *gayatri*, the *gayatri* in *Om* and *Om* in *samadhi*. It is like the sound of a bell: *t-a-m*! The yogi, by following in the trail of the sound *Om*, gradually merges himself with the Supreme *Brahman*.

Om
Brahma kripa hi kevalam
Krishna kripa hi kevalam
Guru kripa hi kevalam
Om Shantih, shantih, shantih!

Kevalam is the ultimate. The ultimate is that which transcends time and space. This is the quality of *Guru-kripa,* which is equated with *Brahma-kripa* and *Krishna-kripa*. Can there be anything higher than the Guru's grace?

Surrender to the Guru

Let me repeat: the Guru asks for nothing; the Guru wants nothing from you. In ancient India, the Gurus lived in ashrams or forest hermitages, where disciples came to live with them, serve them and imbibe knowledge at their feet. But this life of simplicity and service was for the disciple's own benefit and inner growth. This is why our ancient scriptures tell us to give whatever we have to the Guru, while the Guru is enjoined to accept nothing but the disciple's ignorance.

Rishi Yajnavalkya, was King Janaka's Guru. The king asked him how and when he would attain the Highest Reality. His Guru told him about the path of surrender – surrender of body, mind and material wealth. Then and there, King Janaka offered all that he was at the Guru's feet, for his goal was true and lasting peace – *chitta shanti*.

On the following day, King Janaka was in the court participating in a spiritual discussion. A poor Brahmin arrived at the court and begged the king for material assistance to perform the *Upanayanam* (thread ceremony) of his son.

In those days, it was mandatory for the king to offer assistance to poor Brahmins, but Janaka remained silent and unresponsive to the Brahmin's plea.

Repeat *Om* several times in rhythmic synchronization with your breath. Let the rhythm and vibrations of this powerful mantra become one with your breath and your consciousness.

Become aware that you are chanting one of the most sacred sounds on earth. It is the rhythm of existence, the rhythm at the centre of the universe and the energy with which the entire cosmos operates.

Take a deep breath and as you exhale, utter the sacred syllable, *Om*.

O… … … … … ….M.
O… … … … … ….M.
O… … … … … ….M.

As you inhale, breathe in and utter the sacred syllable *Om* silently. Then exhale, and as you breathe out, utter the sacred syllable, *Om* orally, that is, with sound.

Continue chanting. Do not concentrate too much on trying to control your breath. Let your breath flow in and out spontaneously with the chanting.

Breathe in, breathe out; as you inhale, become aware that you are breathing in pure consciousness, that is, bliss. As you exhale, spread this sense of bliss to the world around you.

End your chanting with the Universal Peace prayer: *Om Shanti, Shanti, Shanti!*

FREQUENTLY ASKED QUESTIONS (FAQS)

Question: *The effect of a mantra depends on the number of times it is repeated. Which is the best number – 11, 21, 51 or 108?*
Answer: Repeat the mantra as many times as you can. More important than the number of repetitions is the longing, the yearning that you pour into the repetition.

Question: *I read in a news item that among some* adivasis, *a mantra is used to cure a snakebite. Can this be true?*
Answer: Yes, it is true. The *Siddha* healers of ancient India, too, recited special mantras during the preparation and application of their herbal remedies.

Question: *What makes the recitation of mantras more effective? Is it the sound, word or the meaning?*
Answer: In the case of mantra repetition, first place is given to the sound.

Question: *Do mantras really have healing power?*
Answer: Yes, they do.

Question: *What makes a mantra a mantra? Why are particular lines considered to be filled with special energy as compared to others?*
Answer: As I have already said, words have power. Some words have less power, while others have more. A mantra is a combination of powerful words.

Question: *Why do Gurus give different people different mantras?*

Answer: Every disciple is at a different stage of spiritual evolution and each has a different temperament. Therefore, the Guru gives a mantra according to what he feels is the need of the disciple.

Question: *Is it alright to chant a Buddhist mantra if I am a Hindu?*

Answer: Just as a Hindu can live in a Buddhist neighbour hood, so can he repeat a Buddhist mantra. Mantras transcend considerations of so-called different religions.

Question: *Some say that the* Gayatri *mantra is not to be recited by women. What is your view on this?*

Answer: The *Gayatri* itself is feminine. I think women have a greater right to repeat it than men.

activity. *Tat* is synonymous with the *Brahman,* as it signifies perfection and auspiciousness. *Sat* is also synonymous with the *Brahman* for it denotes the ultimate reality containing all realities. This *mahavakya* has been translated to mean "That which is the Supreme Truth. The Supreme Truth is nothing but *Brahman.* He whom we call God is the universal, fundamental principle of Truth."

Our scriptures say, *Ekam Sat, Vipra Bahudaa Vadanti.* It means that Truth is One but is known by many names. God is the Supreme Truth of truths. Therefore, we say – *Hari Om tat sat*! The paths to Him are as many and as infinite as the stars in the sky. "The Light of all Lights is seated in the hearts of all," says the *Gita.*

How may we attain this great Truth? There is no need to renounce actions, sacrifices, austerities and charity in order to attain the Lord. All that is required is that we submit all these actions to Him, by performing all these activities in worship of God and in the spirit of *arpanam* and surrender, which is done by uttering the Vedic mantra of *Om Tat Sat.* This means that all our actions are done for His sake and we should not expect to gain anything from them. All that we wish is for God to accept them. Therefore, all our activities are purified and sanctified by the dedication: *Om tat sat.*

Om Tat Sat is the *Gita's* mantra. Its repetition is a sacramental act, which opens the doors of grace to us. It is the mantra of faith.

Whatever is done without faith, whether it be an offering (in sacrifice), a gift or austerity, or anything else, is called *asat.* O Arjuna! Such work is of no value hereafter or here.

[XVII: 28]

The sacred Truth of the Lord's Divine Mystery is revealed

Understanding dawned on the visitor who had sought the clarification…

My memory goes back to the golden days, when our beloved Gurudev Sadhu Vaswani lived and moved among us in his physical form. (We believe he is still with us, watching over us, in spirit, even now, nearly 50 years after he has left his physical body.)

One day, he shared with us the story of a good man, who had been afflicted with unbearable pain and agony due to a debilitating illness. The physical suffering that he had to undergo was beyond human endurance. At the height of his affliction, he called out like a lost child, "Dada Shyam! Dada Shyam! Come to my aid!" As you may know, the word *Dada* in Sindhi means elder brother. The call of the distressed man obviously reached the Lord, whom we know to be the very spirit of compassion and love. *Deena bandhu, deena nath* that He is, He responded to the call of the man in pain and believe it or not, the man grew better and was finally cured of his painful condition.

As he was narrating this story to us, Gurudev Sadhu Vaswani urged us to look upon the Lord as our elder Brother. "Call out to Him in love and fraternal affection! Look upon Him as your loving elder Brother! Trust in His loving care and He will never let you down!" Gurudev said to us.

When Gurudev Sadhu Vaswani dropped his physical body, we took to this mantra spontaneously. We had been accustomed to refering to our Gurudev as *Dada,* and it was natural that we should refer to God with the same affectionate and loving terms!

One of the many *bhavas* in the Indian tradition of *bhakti* is the *vatsalya bhava* or the mode of affection for the Lord.

The great saints and Alwars of our country have called out to Lord Krishna as their child, their playmate, their father and friend. We, the members of the Sadhu Vaswani *satsang,* learnt to look upon Him as our elder Brother! When the beautiful mantra *Hare Krishna Hare Ram, Dada Shyam Dada Shyam* is chanted, we feel secure in the protective care and love of the Lord, who is as close to us as our own loving elder brother!

Sage Ribhu and His Disciple

Bhagavan Sri Ramana Maharishi attributed unique value to the lucid exposition of the Supreme Truth in the little-known scripture called the *Ribhu Gita*. The whole scripture is said to represent the teachings given to the Sage Ribhu by God Himself in the form of Lord Shiva. The maharishi is reported to have said that if one repeatedly read the *Ribhu Gita,* one could absorb the Truth of all Being and pass spontaneously into *samadhi* or the natural state of Self-realization. Here is a humorous narrative Ramana Maharishi once told his devotees about Sage Ribhu and his attempts to teach the Supreme Truth to his not-too-bright disciple Nidagha. Although it is a humorous tale, it is a profound parable, which discloses the Highest or Supreme Truth.

Sage Ribhu taught his disciple the Supreme Truth of the One *Brahman* (Pure Consciousness) without a second. However, Nidagha, in spite of his erudition and understanding, did not get sufficient conviction to adopt and follow the path of Self-Knowledge (*Jnana Yoga*), but instead, settled down in his native town to lead a life devoted to the observance of ceremonial religion (*Bhakti Yoga*).

Nevertheless, the Sage loved his disciple as deeply as the latter venerated his master. In spite of his age, Ribhu would visit his disciple in town, just to see how far the latter had evolved, and to see if he had overcome his adherence to mere ritualism. At times, the Sage went in disguise, so that he might observe how Nidagha would act when he was not aware of being observed by his master. On one such occasion, Ribhu, who had disguised himself as a village rustic, found Nidagha intently watching a royal procession. Escaping recognition by town-dweller Nidagha, the village rustic enquired what the bustle was all about, and was told that the king had joined the procession.

"Oh! It is the king! He goes in the procession! But where is he?" asked the rustic.

"There, on the elephant," said Nidagha.

"You say that the king is on the elephant. Yes, I see the two," said the rustic, "but which is the king and which is the elephant?"

"What!" exclaimed Nidagha. "You see the two, but do not know that the man above is the king and the animal below is the elephant? What is the use of talking to a man like you?"

"Pray, be not impatient with an ignorant man like me," begged the rustic. "But you said above and below – what do they mean?"

Nidagha could stand it no more. "You see the king and the elephant, the one above and the other below. Yet you want to know what is meant by 'above' and 'below'?" he burst out. "If things seen and words spoken can convey so little to you, action alone can teach you. Bend forward, bend, I say, and you will know it all too well."

Mantras for All Faiths

A Mantra, is the concentrated expression of the power of the Word and its Sound. The Greek word *logos,* which means 'word, discourse, language, speech or statement', is a highly specialized and complex term in philosophy and religion. Some ancient philosophers actually identified the term with the animating principle of the entire universe. The Neo-Platonic scholar, Philo, used the word to define a Semi-divine being. And, as we all know, the Gospel according to John opens with the statement: "In the beginning was the Word, and the Word was with God, and the Word was God."

This concentrated power and energy associated with the 'Word' finds its best expression in mantras, as we have seen in the earlier chapters of this book. Though the original Sanskrit word *mantra* is essentially associated with the Hindu faith, there are mantras – symbolic statements or groups of powerful words that are special to each faith. They are repeated as prayers, chants, auspicious exclamations and protective devices.

In recent times, there has also been a trend for westerners to adopt the widespread practice of ancient Hindu *abhyasas* like yoga, *pranayama* and meditation. In fact, the calming, stabilizing influence of these techniques is now widely

Om Tat Sat. As you chant in silence, realize that this is a *yajna* that you are performing; not a *yajna* of rites and rituals, but the *yajna* of life, by offering all your thoughts, words and deeds to your Father, Creator and God.

As you continue chanting, realize that all that you are and all that you have is meant to be an offering, an *ahuti* poured into the *havan* that is life. It is also a liberating exercise! Once you have offered all that you are and all that you have to Him, you are free! Free from all worries, fears, anxieties and insecurities!

Continue inhaling and exhaling, following this pattern of chanting. After ten minutes or so, pause to experience detachment of the mind, followed by an inner stillness.

As you feel the inner bliss, dwell on the thought that there is One Absolute Truth and It is all there is!

FREQUENTLY ASKED QUESTIONS (FAQS)

Question: *I am afraid I am a rather materialistic person. I want a compatible mate, a reasonable amount of money, healthy children, etc. These desires make me feel quite guilty. Can I still chant the Name?*
Answer: Yes. You can chant a mantra for any goal that you desire, be it material or spiritual.

Question: *If you chant a mantra in public, will it lose its power?*
Answer: Not necessarily. On the contrary, if you chant the mantra in the company of devotees of God and do *kirtan,* the power of the mantra may actually increase.

Question: *People print sacred mantras on clothes (t-shirts, kurtas, achkan, shawls and caps), post them on walls and*

Prayer which begins with the memorable words, *Our Father,* is an inspiring one to recite, individually and in groups. Just as Hindus recite the *Vedas* in the form of dual chanting, Christians also use the prayer-response format in community recitations. Roman Cathoics recite the *Ave Maria* or *Hail Mary* prayer repeatedly, making a novena or continuous chanting for nine days. *Praise Him!* and *Peace on earth!* are well known and well-loved chants. I must also add that many Indian Christians have incorporated the *pranava* mantra into their prayers, to indicate their cultural affinity to the great ancient scriptures of India. Therefore, we have mantras like *Om Namah Christaya; Om Namah Christave; Yesu Yesu Jai Jai Namo* and *Yesu Christaya Namah.*

Certainly, the most well known of Islamic chants must be the call of the faithful to prayer, sung out in a harmonious melody from every house of worship, five times a day. *Allahu Akbar* (God is Great) is chanted by every devout Muslim in proclamation of the glory of God. *Bismillah Al-Rahman, Al-Rahim* (In the name of Allah, the Compassionate, the Merciful) is an invocation made at the start of every prayer. Many Islamic chants are basically tributes that sing the glory of Allah, the Beneficient and the Merciful.

The Zoroastrians chant the *Yatha Ahu Vairyo* mantra, just as the Hindus chant their *Gayatri* mantra. This prayer is held to be sacred among the Zoroastrians. According to Zoroastrian scriptures, Ahura Mazda uttered this mantra at the dawn of creation and the whole of creation was thus manifested. By chanting it continuously, the Zoroastrians believe that the forces of darkness, present both within and without, can be driven away.

Om Mani Padme Hum is perhaps the most sacred of

Buddhist chants. It is thought that all the teachings of the Buddha are contained in this sacred mantra. It cannot really be translated into a simple phrase or sentence. People believe that chanting this mantra silently or aloud, invokes the powerful benevolent attention and blessings of the Lord who is the very embodiment of compassion. Viewing the written form of the mantra is said to have the same effect. Therefore, we find that the mantra is often carved into stones and placed where people can see them. Spinning the written form of the mantra around in a *Mani wheel,* or prayer wheel, is also thought to confer the same benefit as saying the mantra. These *Mani wheels,* small hand wheels and large wheels with millions of copies of this mantra inside, are found in the temples of many lands, which are influenced by Tibetan Buddhism.

If you have ever entered a Gurudwara for a wedding or a naming ceremony, you would surely have been thrilled by the resonating vibrations of the opening chant of the *Gurbani*:

ek onkar satnam kartapurakh
nirbhao nirvair akaal moorat
ajonee saibhang
guru parsad jap aad sach jugaad sach
hai bhi sach Nanak hosee bhi sach
sochay soch na hovaee
je sochee lakh vaar

This chant, known as the *mool* mantra, recites the glory of the one and only one God, who has infinite qualities and names. He is the same for all religions, and is the Universal Creator, Sustainer and Destroyer. He is manifest everywhere, in every aspect of Creation. He is fearless and without enmity. His form is indestructible. He doesn't need this invocation: *sarve* – all, everyone and every creature that breathes the breath of life. Our rishis were not given to praying for their sect, their caste, their class or indeed, for other Hindus! Narrowness of sectarianism and prejudice against others is alien to the spirit of *sanatana* dharma.

May I say to you, this is not a revolutionary new idea that I am expressing! Our ancient rishis spoke thousands of years ago about the concept of *vasudaiva kutumbakam*, the world as one family. The Tamil Sangam poets of the 3rd Century AD sang, "Every place is my home; everyone is my relative!" No other scripture in the world expresses the spirit of universal brotherhood as beautifully as the *Vedas*:

Om sarvesham swastir bhavatu
Sarvesham shaantir bhavatu
Sarvesham poornam bhavatu
Sarvesham mangalam bhavatu

Auspiciousness be unto all,
Perfect peace be unto all,
Fullness be unto all,
Prosperity be unto all.

Unto all! Unto all! Not unto *me* or unto *us*! This is the great truth that binds us all together as the children of God. We are aspects of the Divine, sparks of the same fire that animates the Universe. Our voices, languages, appearances, skin colours, races and religions may be different, but nothing can take away the great truth that we are all God's children. *Vasudaiva kutumbakam* is a great truth proclaimed by the ancient scriptures of India. Our sages had a truly global vision long before globalization became a catchword!

Let me give you the translation of the entire verse from the *Maha Upanishad*:

> One is my brother and the other is not – this is the thinking of small men or narrow-minded persons. For those who are broad-minded and wise, the entire world is one big family.

When we attain this awareness and enter this realm of light, we will no longer dwell on differences and disharmony; we will begin to bear witness to the truth of God's infinite Power, His infinite Mercy and His infinite Wisdom.

This mantra prays for the health and well-being of all Creation: let none feel the affliction of pain and suffering! This is the true Indian spirit of *maitri* and *daya*. All the great faiths of the world glorify the golden virtue of *daya*, or compassion. *Vaishnav jan to tene kahiye je peer parayi jane re...* You call him who feels the pain of others a true *Vaishnava*.

A Jewish teacher tells us: "Kindness gives to another. Compassion knows no 'other.'" The great Jain tradition of non-violence is rooted in the virtue of compassion. The Buddhist scriptures tell us the story of Ananda, asking the master, "Would it be true to say that the cultivation of loving kindness and compassion is a part of our practice?" To which the Buddha replied, "No. It would not be true to say that the cultivation of love, kindness and compassion is a part of our practice. It would be true to say that the cultivation of loving kindness and compassion is *all* of our practice."

I firmly believe that until we grow in this vision of brotherhood, world peace can never become a reality. "May

How can you ascertain that you have attained to this plane of unity and harmony? Instead of struggling very hard to feel grateful, you will find gratitude welling up spontaneously, like the clear, flowing waters of a mountain spring, from deep within you.

What is more, when you say this mantra at the time of an annoying mishap, after a slip or a fall or after dropping or spilling something, chances are you will feel like laughing out loud, or at least smile as you let go of your habit of stubborn resistance and constant craving for control!

FREQUENTLY ASKED QUESTIONS (FAQS)

Question: *What is the difference between mantras and prayers? Which is the better or more effective of the two?*
Answer: There is a lot of difference between a mantra and a prayer. A prayer is very much like talking to God. In many cases, it comes out from the very depths of the heart. A mantra is the repetition of a word or words we cannot change. If a prayer emerges from the very depths of the heart, its effect can be immediate.

Question: *While reciting mantras, should all doors and windows be closed?*
Answer: It is always better to chant a mantra with the concentration that silence allows. However, you can do it out in the open or in a closed room. No rules are laid down on whether doors and windows should be open or closed.

Question: *Every mantra is said to have a different effect on the body, mind and soul. How can we choose a mantra for ourselves?*
Answer: Until you receive a *Guru* mantra, feel free to repeat any mantra that you feel drawn towards.

Our hearts need to be saturated with love, for love is the light, which will illumine the world. For this, a developed brain is not needed; we need enlightened hearts that can behold the vision of fellowship, unity and brotherhood. Love is what we need to build a new humanity, a new world of brotherhood and peace. We must eliminate the dark forces of greed, selfishness, prejudice and mistrust – and cultivate the power of Love, which is the power of Peace! With this connection made, I would like to share with you the 'Fellowship Song' that I penned a long time ago:

The whole earth is our Country,
And the sky is its dome;
The nations are as mansions
In th' Heavenly Father's Home!

We of China and Japan,
Of 'merica and Ind,
We all are brothers, sisters,—
Of Soviet and Sind!

Hindus, Muslims, Christians, all,
Buddhists and Bahai's,
We share each other's friendship,
And th' love that never dies!

One is the faith we live by:
One is the song we sing!
With little deeds of service
We worship Him our King!

We feed those that are hungry;

- **To reap the benefit of a sacred dip in the holy waters: (purification of the water we use)**

  Gange cha Yamune chaiva Godaavari Saraswati
  Narmade Sindhu Kaaveri jalesmin sannidhim kuru

  May the sacred waters of the Ganga, Yamuna, Godavari, Saraswati, Narmada, Sindhu and Kaveri mingle with this water.

- **Prayer to the Mother for peace and prosperity:**

  Aayur dehi dhanam Dehi
  Vidyaam dehi Maheshwari
  Samastamakhilam dehi
  dehi mey Parameshwari

  Give me long life, give me wealth, give me knowledge, O Maheshwari (Mother Goddess), O Parmeshwari, give me all that I desire.

- **Prayer to Dhanvantri, the God of Healing and Medicine:**

  Om Namo Bhagavate
  Maha Sudharshana
  Vasudevaya Dhanvantraye;
  Amrutha Kalasa Hasthaaya
  Sarva Bhaya Vinasaaya
  Sarva Roka Nivaranaya
  Thrilokya Pathaye
  Thrilokya Nithaye
  Sri Maha Vishnu Swarupa
  Sri Dhanvantri Swarupa
  Sri Sri Sri
  Aoushata Chakra Narayana Swaha

We pray to the God, who is known as Sudarshana Vasudeva Dhanvantri. He holds the *Kalasha* full of the nectar of immortality. Lord Dhanvantri removes all fears and all diseases. He is the well wisher and the preserver of the three worlds. Dhanvantri is an aspect of Lord Vishnu, empowered to heal the *Jivatmas*. We bow to the Lord of Ayurveda.

- **Prayer to Lord Rama for quick relief from danger and distress:**

Om Aapadam apahartaaram Daataram Sarva Sampadaam
Lokaabhi Ramam Sri Ramam Bhuyo Bhuyo Namaamyaham

I bow again and again to Lord Rama, who removes all obstacles and dangers, who grants all wealth and pleases all people.

- **Mantra to cultivate Cosmic Consciousness:**

Om purnam-adah purnam-idam purnat purnam-udachyate
Purnasya purnam-aadaya purnam-eva-avasisyate

The invisible Cosmic Power is whole and infinite; the visible universe is infinite; the infinite whole (universe) appears out of the infinite whole (Cosmic Power); when the infinite whole (universe) is subtracted from the infinite whole (Cosmic Power), what remains is still infinite and whole and perfect! (Cosmic Power)

Love your friends and love your enemies. I look forward to the day – may that day come soon in the life of everyone of you – when you can honestly say, "We have no enemies! All are our friends!"

Sri Ramanuja and the Sacred Mantra of Liberation

When we read about the life of Sri Ramanuja, we are profoundly moved by the humility and persistence with which he sought initiation from one of his great Gurus, Gosthi Purna, who was also known after his place of residence as Thirukkottiyur Nambi (The sage of Thirukkottiyur).

When Ramanuja was first directed by one of his mentors to go to Purna for initiation into the sacred mantra of Liberation, he walked all the way to Thirukkottiyur, where he prostrated himself at Purna's feet and beseeched him, "Teach me the holy doctrine, Sire!"

Purna was determined to test Ramanuja's strength of faith, his perseverance and his devotion. In an off-hand manner, he said to Ramanuja, "What have I to tell, and to whom?" he turned his face away, giving Ramanuja no countenance.

Without a word and without reproach, Ramanuja prostrated himself before the Guru and then turned to walk back the way he came.

Sri Ramanuja sought his Guru's grace not once, not twice, but 18 times, walking all the way from Srirangam to Thirukkottiyur to obtain knowledge of the mantra that wife of Lord Vishnu, I bow to you. Please forgive me for touching you with my feet.

- **When lighting the lamp before your daily prayer:**

  Shubham karoti kalyaanam aarogyam dhana sampada
  Shatrubuddhi vinaashaya deepajyothi namostuthe

  Just like the light from this lamp, spread happiness, prosperity and health in our lives. Just as the light rids us of darkness, get rid of our ignorance.

- **Mantra at the start of a learning session:**

  Om saha naavavatu sahanau bhunaktu
  sahaveeryam karavaavahai
  Tejaswi naavadheetamastu maa vid vishaa vahai
  om shaanthih shaanthih shaanthih

  May He protect all, may He nurture all, may we all perform together the most heroic and *divine* actions; may our learning be prosperous to all; may we never quarrel on the different beliefs we may have; may we illuminate together, may we live in harmony. May there be peace for all and for ever.

- **Mantras to your *ishta devata:***

  Om Sri Maha Ganapataye Namah
  Om Namah Shivaya
  Om Namo Bhagavate Vaasudevaya
  Om Sri Raamaya Namah
  Om Sri Durgaya Namah
  Om Sri Maha Lakshmyai Namah
  Om Krishnaya Namah

be the birthright of every true believer to know the secret of moksha?

On receiving the mantra, Ramanuja immediately climbed up to the top of the steeple of the temple tower at Thrukkottiyur and summoned devotees of all castes and creeds to assemble before the temple. From the temple tower, he proclaimed to the large gathering of people assembled there, the purport of the instruction. By some accounts, he literally shouted out the sacred mantra at the top of his voice, so that everyone could hear the same and reap the benefits of eternal bliss!

Yes! Contrary to the injunction of the Guru, Sri Ramanuja broke his pledge of secrecy and proclaimed the Divine mantra from the temple tower, so that the whole of mankind may adopt it to achieve liberation! When Purna learnt that Sri Ramanuja had broken his vow, he was shocked and angry. He repeated his earlier admonition, "You will go to hell for your disobedience."

Bowing down in deep reverence to the Guru, the Acharya replied, "My beloved Guru, I humbly accept your punishment! I will gladly consent to go to hell, for it will benefit thousands of others, who can attain salvation with the help of the sacred mantra!"

Purna was a true Guru. Profoundly moved by Ramanuja's selfless devotion and compassion, he embraced his extraordinary disciple and freely forgave him, blessing him in his efforts to lead one and all to Liberation!

The great Acharya, thus demonstrated in thought, word and deed, the true spirit of *sarve bhavantu sukinaha.*

JAICO PUBLISHING HOUSE

Elevate Your Life. Transform Your World.

ESTABLISHED IN 1946, Jaico Publishing House is home to world-transforming authors such as Sri Sri Paramahansa Yogananda, Osho, the Dalai Lama, Sri Sri Ravi Shankar, Sadhguru, Robin Sharma, Deepak Chopra, Jack Canfield, Eknath Easwaran, Devdutt Pattanaik, Khushwant Singh, John Maxwell, Brian Tracy, and Stephen Hawking.

Our late founder Mr. Jaman Shah first established Jaico as a book distribution company. Sensing that independence was around the corner, he aptly named his company Jaico ('Jai' means victory in Hindi). In order to service the significant demand for affordable books in a developing nation, Mr. Shah initiated Jaico's own publications. Jaico was India's first publisher of paperback books in the English language.

While self-help, religion and philosophy, mind/body/spirit, and business titles form the cornerstone of our non-fiction list, we publish an exciting range of travel, current affairs, biography, and popular science books as well. Our renewed focus on popular fiction is evident in our new titles by a host of fresh young talent from India and abroad. Jaico's recently established translations division translates selected English content into nine regional languages.

Jaico distributes its own titles. With its headquarters in Mumbai, Jaico has branches in Ahmedabad, Bangalore, Chennai, Delhi, Hyderabad, and Kolkata.

SINCE 1946

mantra with faith and devotion, your life may actually change for the better and acquire a new radiance.

Question: *Isn't it limiting God to call Him by a name?*
Answer: The Name Divine does not in any way limit God! In fact, nothing that we may say or do can limit God in any way. God is the Nameless one, though the sages have called Him by many names. You may call Him by any name you like, but none can describe Him completely. He is beyond and above the Names by which the sages have called Him. In the presence of God, man becomes speechless. No words can fully express the greatness and glory of God; each Name has its own value and power. Each Name is an aspect of the Whole, Perfect and Eternal One!

Question: *To chant mantras, do I have to be a vegetarian?*
Answer: No. But it is helpful to be a vegetarian, because vegetarian food is *saatvic.*

The Mantra for all Disciples

Gurur Brahma, Gurur Vishnu
Gurur Devo Maheshwarah
Guruh Saakshaat Parabrahma
Tasmai Sri Gurave Namah

While I have referred to all other mantras in this book by the names of the deities to whom they are addressed, the naming pattern for this mantra changes. This mantra expresses our adoration and devotion to the Guru. I choose to call it a mantra for disciples, because it stresses a disciple's sense of belonging to the Guru; indeed, it establishes his loving right as a disciple of the Guru.

There is yet another point that I would like to make: if there is one thing that God wants from us, His creatures, it is our love and devotion. Lord Krishna urges us again and again in the *Gita*: "Surrender to me, offer your life and actions to me: practice devotion to me." He wants us to approach Him in love and devotion, for the gift that he alone can bestow on us, the Gift of Liberation.

The Guru desires nothing in return! The Guru is the great cleanser, a great purifier, not just a great teacher. Caught in the web of maya, caught in the snare of sense-desires and worldly pleasures, we accumulate bad karma, birth after

Here is another interesting sloka that tells us about the exalted status of the Guru:

Gurur pita Gurur mata
Gurur Daivam gurur-gatih:
Sive ruste gurustrata
Gurau rasti na kaschana

> The Guru is father, the Guru is mother, the Guru is God, the Guru is the refuge. If Shiva becomes angry, the Guru will intercede on your behalf; if the Guru is angry, you will be without help.

What a great promise is made to us here! If we should ever sin or displease God with our evil ways, we do not have to face His wrath or offer our pathetic explanations to Him; the Guru will cleanse, purify, forgive and release us from our error. But if we should offend the Guru, where can we turn? We could go to God, but He Himself will direct us to the Guru for forgiveness and redemption!

Whoever you are, whatever you may be, whatever you may possess, no matter what your reputation, virtue and other merits – these are all of no avail to you without the grace of a Guru. You cannot attain salvation or achieve self-realization without absolute devotion to the Guru. I leave the final words on this subject to Sri Adi Shankara:

> The Supreme Lord moved by the reverential homage of his devotees, incarnates, out of compassion, into the form of a Guru. Thereby, He comes within the ambit of our sight, freely transmits to us the wisdom of ultimate Reality and enables us to cross over this sorrowful *sansar sagar* – the ocean of worldly life.